A.D. 2000

Books by Rene Noorbergen

A.D. 2000—A Book about the End of Time
Treasures of the Lost Races
Living with Loss
The $10,000,000 Hostage
The Death Cry of an Eagle
Nostradamus—Invitation to a Holocaust
Secrets of the Lost Races
The Soul Hustlers
Programmed to Live
The Ark File
Charisma of the Spirit
Glossolalia—Sweet Sounds of Ecstasy
Ellen G. White—Prophet of Destiny
You Are Psychic
Jeane Dixon—My Life & Prophecies

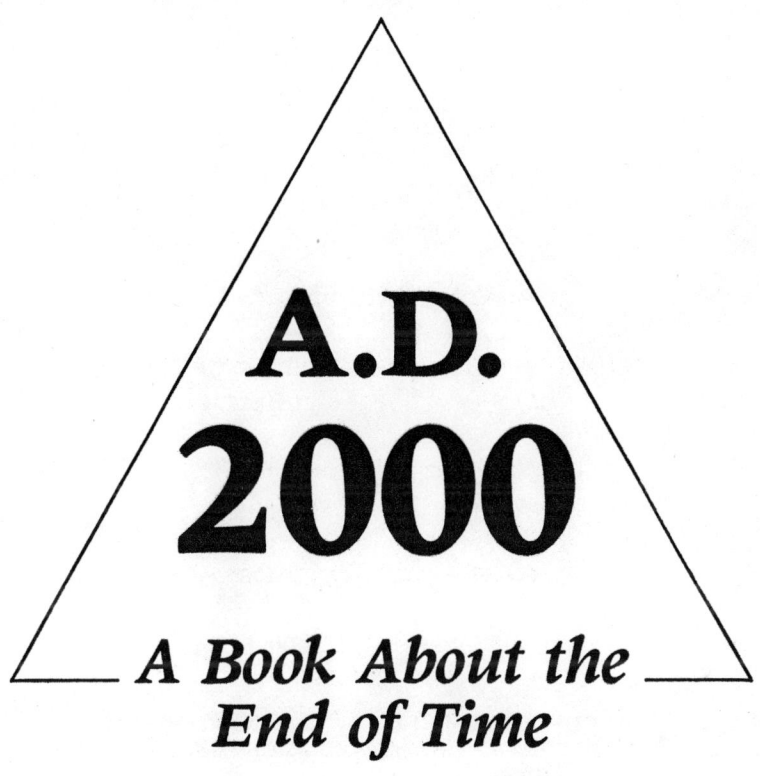

A.D. 2000

A Book About the End of Time

by
Rene Noorbergen

THE BOBBS-MERRILL COMPANY, INC.
INDIANAPOLIS / NEW YORK

COPYRIGHT © 1984 by Rene Noorbergen
All rights reserved.
No part of this publication may be reproduced, stored in a retrieval system, or transmitted in any form or by any means, mechanical, electronic, photocopying, recording or otherwise, without the prior written permission of the publisher. For information, address The Bobbs-Merrill Co., Inc., 630 Third Avenue, New York, NY 10017.

Published by The Bobbs-Merrill Co., Inc.
Indianapolis/New York
Manufactured in the United States of America
First Printing
Designed by Jacques Chazaud

Library of Congress Cataloging in Publication Data

Noorbergen, Rene.
  A.D. 2000

    1. Prophecies. 2. End of the world. I. Title.
II. Title: AD two thousand.
BF1809.N66   1984   133.3'24   83–15594
ISBN 0–672–52769–3

A WORD OF APPRECIATION

To Robert Surridge for the hours of research he put into one of the pivotal chapters of the book;

And to Charles Bulterman and KLM Royal Dutch Airlines for introducing me to their Atlanta–Amsterdam connection—speeding up the research beyond measure!

To the One who will bring final fulfillment of all dreams
and the total cessation of all strife
this book is dedicated.

November 9, 1983

CONTENTS

Introduction xi

1. A.D. 2,000: Time of the End? 1
2. The Rise of the Last World Leader 11
3. Michael and Jeane: Prophets of Doom or Hope? 35
4. Storehouse of Anger Spilling Over 59
5. The Far-Reaching Visions of John of Patmos 101
6. Humanity's Rush to Judgment 125
7. Armageddon: The End of Time? 141

Epilogue 151

Bibliography 153

Index 157

Introduction

Ever since George Orwell's *1984* was published shortly after the end of World War II, some have tremblingly held their white surrender flags in readiness while still others began to feel the pangs of fright and a paralyzing sense of anxiety. For if there is one single thing humanity does not need at this point in time, it is total and absolute government control all the way from the cradle to the grave.

Of course, we can all take solace in the knowledge that the suppressive society so ably forecast by George Orwell was nothing but a dream. A writer's nightmare!

But don't believe for a moment that the danger is past.

Orwell's "vision"—if that's what it may be called—was merely a hint of what's in store for us. In many ways our "dream" has already bypassed his. We have begun to construct our own ghoulish nightmare and are carefully superimposing it on our own future, and by the time we have covered every aspect of our lives and have perfected our evil scheme, the allotted time for the human race may have run out.

One does not have to be a soothsayer or be endowed with psychic intuition to find himself in the same league with King Belshazzar of Ancient Babylon and recognize the doomsday message in the handwriting on the wall. We live within a troubled time slot and most of it is of our own making. We have passed through two major world wars and are treading water on a globe that has not known one day of peace in several thousand years. There's always a war being fought *somewhere*. Starvation in the Third World has reached an all-time high. Earthquakes, volcanic eruptions, social unrest, revolutions, disease epidemics, annihilation of plant and animal life and stories about man's capability for wholesale destruction are crowding the nation's headlines. But it seems that we may well be traveling on a preordained path where the cobblestones have been etched with the end-time predictions left there by the ancient prophets who went before us.

There is a dire foreboding of destiny in what we do, and in some ways it rekindles the old question, "Does it happen because it has been prophesied or was it prophesied because it was known that it would happen?"

Though we will never know the answer, the correlation between prophecy and the forceful cadence of world events is so strong that we can only find a way out of our manmade dilemma by turning to and relying on the words of the ancient prophets.

Of all the prophetic passages that describe our day, those found in the Book of Matthew, Chapter 24, are most accurate in forecasting our times. But most encouraging is that it does not stop with prophesying the problems but also marks the way for escape. Its logical sequence of calamities ends with the introduction of a period where all strife will cease and a New Age will be heralded in by the coming of the Man of Peace.

How will it happen and exactly when will it take place?

Will *A.D. 2000* really be the target year for the fulfillment of the Drama of the Ages?

Introduction

The compilation of material found on the following pages is the result of open-ended research but points nevertheless to a climactic end of a globe that has been tormented by its human occupants. Lee A. Dubridge, once commented, "Our spacecraft called Earth is reaching its capacity." He might just as well have said that man's destructive nature has finally caught up with him, for we have obviously reached the "point of no return."

It's 1984 and mankind is running scared.

We can only hope that the prophecies for A.D. 2000, though frightening, will bring some perspective to a species evolving away from a peaceful vision of its own.

Rene Noorbergen
April 20, 1984

1
A.D. 2000: Time of the End?

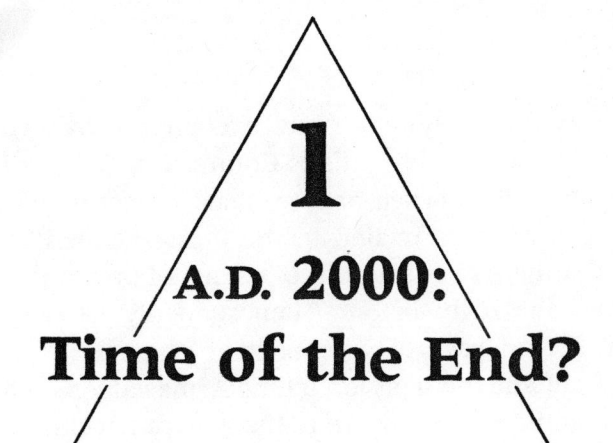

> And the sixth angel poured out his vial upon the great river Euphrates; and the water thereof was dried up that the way of the kings in the east might be prepared.
> And he gathered them together into a place called in the Hebrew tongue Armageddon.
> And there came a great voice out of the temple of heaven from the throne, saying It is done!
>
> —Rev. 16:12, 16, 17

The world we live in is a frightening one, and the fear of the future that has been expressed in every nation on the earth is now beginning to echo in the highest echelons.

President Ronald Reagan first let his deep concern about the future spill over during a private meeting on October

18, 1983, with Thomas Dine, executive director of the American-Israel Public Affairs Committee.

Profoundly shocked and troubled by the massacre of American Marines in Beirut, the President mentioned to Dine that he had talked to the parents of one of the killed Marines the night before. Then suddenly he said, "You know, I turn back to your ancient prophets in the Old Testament and the signs foretelling Armageddon, and I find myself wondering if—if we're the generation that is going to see that come about. I don't know if you've noted any of those prophecies lately, but, believe me, they certainly describe the times we're going through."

Whatever anyone's judgment may be about the American President, he is certainly not a religious fanatic. To hear of his concern about the biblical prophecies and to learn that he has considered world power politics in the light of the words of the ancient prophets makes one realize that he is very human indeed, for he was merely uttering the fears and anxieties shared by millions of people the world over.

Let's make no mistakes about it. There are significant political and spiritual changes in the wind, and when President Reagan voiced his worries about the destiny of our planet, he shared not only his spiritual concerns but the emotional struggles of a Commander in Chief of the armed forces as well.

As someone said after reading his remarks, "What does he know that we don't? What is he really hiding from us?"

The trouble is that there is not much to hide anymore.

There exists in the world today a growing concern about a future catastrophe of gigantic proportions and the world's slim chances of surviving it. Considering our present destructive tendencies and capabilities, our seemingly unending social upheaval, the waxing brutality of one individual against another, the still developing sexual revolution, the rise of the chemical generation, not to mention our attempts to duplicate the feats of Creation through genetic engineering in the sterile laboratories of the land, it does appear that we are indeed heading for a final showdown.

The concerned people of the world feel that we are all on the threshold of something awesome. They fear that by the time all the facts are in and we human beings, with our increasing inhumanity, have reached the apex of our capabilities, we may also have reached the end of life.

Much of the world's mounting uneasiness springs from the thought that the fingers touching the nuclear buttons may tremble just once too often. In minutes our beautiful blue and green planet can be transformed into a hellish nightmare of primeval heat with no winners and no survivors.

Already we have arrived at the stage in our social and moral development where an end-of-the-world-obsession has captured our imaginations. Though we bravely explore it in our books, radio and television programs, and motion pictures, our wish is to purge the fear. Yet our science-fiction writers sound more like apocalyptic soothsayers as time goes by.

We must do something to change our course. The time is past when we could stick our heads into the sands of ignorance, like the proverbial ostrich, hoping, trusting, that all of our problems will have vanished by the time we have to come up for air.

Neither the ostrich nor we can win that way.

In the research I have conducted over the years in connection with the books I have written, I have discovered that fear of the future is not a burden peculiar to twentieth-century humanity. The specific stresses we who are living today feel about our future may be as characteristic of us as our technological advances, yet the anxiety is not a new phenomenon. Practically every generation since the dawn of time has given voice to its mounting concern and has lived in quiet fear of the unknown tomorrow. People past and present share the instinctive feeling that someday there will come a crisis that will ultimately destroy both humanity and this planet.

When combing the records of the ancients, one finds that the prophecies dealing with the end of the world are as old as humanity itself. We find the stunning fear of the end of the world running through these ancient works like an unbroken chain. It is there in the writings of the Egyptian magician Hermes Trismegistus, in the Ragnarok of the Norsemen, and in other works, from the mysterious pronouncements of the Sibylline oracles to the celestial forebodings of the Renaissance.

Anxiety about the future is, of course, not at all uncommon; human beings are usually fearful of the unknown. What is significant about these fears, however, is that they have found expression in predictions of a major world catastrophe offered by psychic seers and biblical prophets over a period of several thousand years. But more alarming is that they predicted the end of the world and of human history not in their lifetime, but toward the end of a historical period that can be identified as the second millennium A.D. Our time!

Why all of them would zero in on approximately the same time period is perhaps one of the most perplexing questions of all. Yet at this moment we are living in the predicted time slot during which their prophecies are racing toward fulfillment. If we are to believe them, then we have less than twenty years left before the events of history will catch up with their final prophecies, dropping us on the threshold of the long expected drama of the ages.

Psychic phenomena have become big business, and some eager practitioners have capitalized on people's fear of the unknown.

A.D. 2000: Time of the End?

A Roper survey conducted in the United States in 1974 revealed that at that time approximately 53 percent of the population believed in supernatural phenomena and psychic manifestations and predictions. I have no doubt that the percentage of believers is even higher in Great Britain.

A number of years ago I conducted a special survey of fifty leading American psychic practitioners as part of a major research project. In the course of that work, I discovered that the predictions of modern-day "prophets" are gaining more acceptance with each passing year, and that the forecasts about the "time of the end" are the most sought-after of all.

Take their predictions and back them up with the thus far infallible record of biblical prophecy, the realistic evaluations of military strategists, and the reports of scientists who have studied the atmospheric consequences of a nuclear war, and the mere feeling that something is due to happen will soon change into the harsh realization that life on this planet as we know it is about to come to an end—and all because humanity has not been able to control its hatred, jealousy, and greed.

A short while ago I found myself deeply engaged in a rather heated political discussion with a leading member of the Palestine Liberation Army in Amman, Jordan. Our disagreement had centered on the uncertain future of the volatile region, when my excitable companion suddenly stopped and turned.

For a moment he sat there, silently observing the stream of foreign dignitaries who had wandered into the lobby of the Intercontinental Hotel, and watched their angry and discouraged gestures as they began to discuss the result of the meeting they had just attended.

Their frustration and disgust must have been contagious, for the scowl abruptly left his face, and following the example of his Arab brothers, he, too, threw up his hands.

"What's the use of all this rhetoric?" he snarled bitterly, obviously referring to our political discussion. "Allah is going to do it his way anyway!"

Not only did this unexpected reaction terminate our discussion about the future of the Middle East, but with this one remark he had admitted that much of what we all face is totally unchangeable and probably the result of predestination.

There is indeed little doubt that we have become unwilling but indispensable players in a cosmic poker game. A game with high stakes and even higher risks. A game in which even the winner will be merely a survivor.

The situation was clear one hundred twenty-two years ago to Henry Adams, a young American who worked with the United States legation in London. Proud of the progress of science, yet worried about what it might eventually do to the human race, he wrote to his brother:

> I tell you these are great times. Man has mounted science, and is now run away with. I firmly believe that before many centuries more, science will be the master of man. The engines he will have invented will be beyond his strength to control. Some day science may have the existence of mankind in its power, and the human race will commit suicide by blowing up the world.

Forty-seven years later in his book *Interpretation of Radium*, the chemist Frederick Soddy, commenting on ancient accounts of mysterious explosions, said something very similar: "Can we not read in them some justification for the belief that some former forgotten race of men attained not only to the knowledge we have so recently won, but also to the power that is not yet ours?" he asked. "I believe that there have been civilizations in the past," he continued soberly, "that were familiar with atomic energy, and that by misusing it they were totally destroyed."

Humanity has never been able to learn from its own confused past, and history does indeed contain references to a previous holocaust.

Perhaps this was what Robert Oppenheimer, the father of the A-bomb, had in mind when, during a lecture at the University of Rochester, he gave a somewhat enigmatic answer to a student who had asked whether the bomb that was exploded at Alamogordo, New Mexico, in 1945 during the Manhattan Project was the first one to be detonated.

The physicist hesitated for a moment and then replied carefully, "Well, yes. In modern times, of course."

He may have had in mind a record of a detonation in ancient times, which first came to light in the nineteenth century during the British imperial rule of India. At that time, European scholars had begun their first examination of the *Mahabharata,* a great Indian epic of 200,000 lines, dating back in its present form to 500 B.C. The scholars soon realized that they were dealing with a very ancient work indeed, for textual evidence indicated that the events referred to in the epic poem took place one to two thousand years earlier—probably somewhere between 2500 to 2700 B.C.

For a while the many references to flying craft and fearsome weapons of fiery destruction were considered nothing more than poetic hyperbole. In the words of one Victorian commentator, V. R. Dikshitar, "Everything in this literature is imagination and should be summarily dismissed as unreal." But after the initial research into radiation and nuclear physics at the turn of the century, there were already those who saw in the *Mahabharata* and other ancient legends references to a use of energy modern scientists were just beginning to understand.

The *Mahabharata* describes an eighteen-day war between the Kauravas and the Pandavas, who inhabited the upper regions of the Ganges. Not long after this war, a second battle was waged against the Vrishnis and Andhakas in the same region.

In the *Mahabharata* one finds a description of a terrifying weapon:

> The valiant Adwattan, remaining steadfast in his Vimana, landed upon the water and from there unleashed the Agneya weapon, incapable of being resisted by the very gods.
>
> Taking careful aim against his foes, the preceptor's son let loose the blazing missile of smokeless fire with tremendous force.
>
> Dense arrows of flame, like a great shower, issued forth upon creation, encompassing the enemy. Meteors flashed down from the sky. A thick gloom swiftly settled upon the Pandava hosts. All points of the compass were lost in darkness. Fierce winds began to blow. Clouds roared upward, showering dust and gravel.
>
> Birds croaked madly, and beasts shuddered from the destruction. The very elements seemed disturbed. The sun seemed to waver in the heavens. The earth shook, scorched by the terrible violent heat of this weapon.
>
> Elephants burst into flame and ran to and fro in a frenzy, seeking protection from the terror. Over a vast area, other animals crumpled to the ground and died. The waters boiled, and the creatures residing therein also died.

> From all points of the compass the arrows of flame rained continuously and fiercely. The missile of Adwattan burst with the power of thunder, and the hostile warriors collapsed like trees burnt in a raging fire. Thousands of war vehicles fell down on all sides.

The description of the second weapon is even more frightening than the first:

> Ghurka, flying in his swift and powerful Vimana, hurled against the three cities of the Vrishnis and Andhakas a single projectile charged with all the power of the Universe.
>
> An incandescent column of smoke and fire, as brilliant as ten thousand suns, rose in all its splendor. It was the Unknown Weapon, the iron thunderbolt, a gigantic messenger of death which reduced to ashes the entire race of the Vrishnis and Andhakas.
>
> The corpses were so burnt they were no longer recognizable. Hair and nails fell out. Pottery broke without cause. Birds, disturbed, circled in the air and were turned white. Foodstuffs were poisoned. To escape, the warriors threw themselves in streams to wash themselves and their equipment....
>
> With the destruction ended, the Kuru king Yudistthira, was informed of the power of the iron thunderbolt and the slaughter of the Vrishnis.

We could attribute these descriptions to the overactive imagination of some unknown Hindu sage of long ago, but there are too many details that make this account unnervingly similar to an eyewitness report of an atomic explosion: the brightness of the blast, the column of rising smoke and fire, the fallout, the intense heat and shock waves, the appearance of the victims, and the effects of radiation poisoning.

Hindu scholars believe that these ancient atomic explosions occurred between 3102 and 2449 B.C. They were able to figure this out from the detailed astronomical configuration given in connection with the battles in the *Mahabharata*.

The exact date of the detonations may be in doubt, but their occurrence is not, for evidence of vitrified soil and fused and glazed ruins can be found throughout the Far East and in Southern Iraq, the Sahara Desert, the Lofoten Islands of Norway, and even in Scotland and Ireland where the granite along the coast shows evidence of having been melted to a depth of one foot. Only atomic explosions could have generated sufficient heat to cause such destruction.

A human skeleton with a radioactivity level fifty times greater than normal has been found in the Ganges area, and others were discovered in Pakistan in what used to be known as the Indus Valley of India. There, among the ruined remains of the ancient cities of Mohenjo-Daro and Harappa, archaeologists have discovered skeletons that show a radioactivity level equal to that found in the human remains of Hiroshima and Nagasaki.

Need more be said?

Both nuclear physicists and military strategists are fully aware of the devastation caused by these destructive devices. They once destroyed entire civilizations. Who or what will destroy ours?

2
The Rise of the Last World Leader

> We seem to be moving, drifting, steadily against our will, against the will of every race, and every people, and every class, toward some hideous catastrophe. Everyone wishes to stop it, but they do not know how.
>
> —Winston Churchill

In doing my research and my subsequent evaluations of the anticipated course of humanity's future, I have encountered many surprises. Among the most startling are the forecasts that the Soviet Union will make an about-face and that its people will regain their religious freedom as a prelude to the end of the world.

According to some of the great psychics, the bloodthirsty Russian Bear will somehow be transformed into a lamb and will eventually become one of the leading spiritual powers on this globe. The seers regard this as one of the final events before the last great war.

The "sleeping seer" of Kentucky, Edgar Cayce, one of the greatest psychic prophets of the twentieth century, claimed that we are at present entering a period when humanity will experience what may be called a "spiritual rebirth," a period of "spiritual cooperation" that will slowly but certainly affect all nations. Prophesying at the height of the aggressive power of Joseph Stalin, he foretold a Christianization of the Russian Communist state. Furthermore he predicted that Russia's new Christians would become a major force in the return of the human race to traditional religious values. He stressed that this change would come after the fall of the Communist regime and that Russia's spiritual change would affect not only the Soviet Union but also the nations of Western Europe. His visions convinced him that the spiritualization that would begin in Russia would eventually influence affairs in the United States, France, England, Japan, and China as well.

The Kentucky seer's vision was almost identical to the prediction given to the three children of Fatima, Portugal, in 1917. A miraculous being, believed by many to be the Virgin Mary, appeared to the children bearing the message that the great war in progress at that time would soon end. But she went on to warn that if humanity continued to offend God, another more terrible war would ensue. To prevent this, she expressed to the children her wish that Russia be consecrated to the Immaculate Heart. "If this is not done," she sternly warned, "then the next war will be followed by a difficult time during which Russia will spread her 'errors' around the globe, causing the church to undergo great persecution." She did, however, end her vision with a measure of hope, emphasizing that, in the end, Russia would be converted.

Even Nostradamus, the great French seer, foresaw this change in Russia, for in 1555 he wrote these prophetic words:

> The Law of More will be seen to decline:
> After another much more seductive
> Dnieper first will come to give way
> Through gifts another appealing, more attractive.
>   (III:95)

> At the places and times when there is a religious abstinence [Lent],
> The Communist law will be opposed.
> The old leaders will strongly support it but they will be removed from power,
> Loving of Everything in Common [communism] to suffer a significant setback. (IV:32)

> From the Slavic people will come songs, slogans and threats,
> But then their Leaders and Statesmen placed in prisons,
> The pronouncements of these headless idiots
> Will be received as divine utterances. (I:14)

A major point made here by Nostradamus is that at some time during an Easter season, there will be a major upheaval in the government of the Soviet Union. Rising demands for consumer goods as produced in capitalist nations, combined with a resurgence of old-fashioned nationalism among the minorities absorbed by the USSR, will force the old Stalinist dictators from the Kremlin. It will result in the establishment of a new form of government that will be Communist in name only.

A more detailed explication of Nostradamus's first line would be, "The Law of More will be seen to decline," referring to the philosophy of Sir Thomas More, as found in his *Utopia*, published in Latin in 1516 and undoubtedly read by Nostradamus while he was still a schoolboy. Any of the psychic's contemporaries would undoubtedly connect the "Law of More" with socialism. Many prominent literary sources classify More's *Utopia* along with Plato's *Republic* and the writings of Bacon as the literary ancestors of the modern ideology of communism.

Edgar Leoni is quoted in Steward Robb's *Strange Prophecies That Came True* as follows:

> For the reader in the second half of the 20th century, this is one of the most interesting of all the prophecies of Nostradamus—one full of potent meaning for this era, after having had none from the 16th to the 20th century. We now have the generic name "communism" to apply to the Utopian ideologies of which Sir Thomas More's *Utopia* is the common ancestor. . . . The prophecy implies a widespread success of this ideology prior to its decline, and mentions that the decline will start where the Dnieper is located. This is the principal river of the Ukraine. In Nostradamus's day it was one of the most backward parts of Europe, part of the Polish-Lithuanian state for three hundred years, and hardly an area Nostradamus would choose for the locale involving any contemporary movement of this nature, such as the Anabaptists. Accordingly, it is not unreasonable to speculate on a possible 20th-century fulfillment of this

The Rise of the Last World Leader

prophecy, involving the Soviet Ukraine and perhaps its chief city (which is on the Dnieper), Kiev. The nature of the more seductive and the more attractive tongue are subjects for further speculation.

From the context of the verse, one can infer that this ideology would not remain a theory but would eventually be put into practice and enjoy some degree of acceptance before, as the first line reads, More's law "will be seen to decline." The twentieth-century fulfillment of the first part of this prediction—with a full one-third of the world today living under some form of communism—needs no elaboration.

A surprising element in this prognostication of Nostradamus is his designation of the place where the future decline of communism is to take place. "The Boristhenes first will come to give way," he proclaimed unhesitantly. The river that used to be known as the Boristhenes is the modern Dnieper, one of the three prominent rivers of the Ukraine. Not even in his wildest dreams could Karl Marx have imagined that this backward area of the Soviet Union would be the first to experiment with proletarian dictatorship. But this is exactly what eventually happened.

Nostradamus's use of the Dnieper may have meant any one of several things. Today the Ukraine is one of Russia's most troublesome regions, peopled by an extremely nationalistic race whose uncompromising adherence to Ukrainian custom cannot be controlled by the Soviet regime. It perhaps will be the Ukrainians who will initiate a second Russian revolution. It is also possible however, that the psychic used the Dnieper as a synecdoche to represent Russia as a whole. Kiev, once the capital of Russia, is situated on the banks of the Dnieper, and perhaps equally important is the fact that the headwaters of the river are in the Valdai Hills in the Smolensk region, not all that far from Moscow. Consequently, whether we use sixteenth-century terminology or twentieth-century words, the seer's use of the Boristhenes appears to symbolize the area that is now known as the Soviet Union.

History has recorded the words of another seer of the Middle Ages, a woman known as Mother Shipton, who often predicted the future of England. Pointing her psychic finger at the last days of the human race, she offered this prediction:

> When women dress like men and trousers wear
> And cut off all their locks of hair,
> When pictures look alive with movements free
> When ships like fishes swim beneath the sea,
> When men outstripping birds can soar the sky,
> Then half the world, deep drenched in blood,
>   shall die.

The changes predicted for this world in a time period that most of the old seers have pinpointed as the twentieth century are earthshaking indeed, and the forecasts dealing with the spiritual changes and the eventual arrival of a "Man of Peace" have permeated all prophetic thought for thousands of years. It has always been felt that a deep religious awakening in some of the major nations and a resulting ecumenism among the world's major religions would be a natural development around this time.

The visions and revelations indicating the appearance of this Man of Peace come from some surprising sources. The Eastern religions, for example, have an abundance of them.

Before his death, Prince Siddhartha, Gautama Buddha, the founder of what is probably the most common religion in the East, prophesied that his work would be continued by such a man:

The Rise of the Last World Leader

> I am not the first Buddha who has come upon earth, nor shall I be the last. In due time another Buddha will rise in the world, a Holy One, a supremely enlightened one, endowed with wisdom auspicious, embracing the Universe, an incomparable Leader of Men, a ruler of gods and mortals.
>
> He will reveal to you the same eternal truths which I have taught you.
>
> He will establish his Law, glorious in its origin, glorious at the climax and glorious at the goal in the Spirit and the Letter.
>
> He will proclaim a righteous life life wholly perfect and pure, such as I now proclaim. His disciples will number many thousands while mine number many hundreds.
>
> He will be known as Maitreya.

Gautama Buddha further predicted that when the Maitreya (the World Unifier) comes, he and his band of close associates and followers will come to the East from the West (meaning the Middle East).

The prophecies concerning the Maitreya have naturally spread far beyond the boundaries of India and Pakistan, and several explorers who traveled through Central Asia to gather bits of folklore and ancient tradition have repeatedly come across references to the coming of this Buddha reincarnation.

> First will begin an unprecedented war of all the nations. And Brother shall rise against Brother. It will result in the flow of oceans of blood, and the understanding between the people shall cease to exist. Even the meaning of the word "teacher" shall be forgotten. But at that time the teachers shall appear, and they will preach the True

Teaching in all the world. People will be drawn to this word of Truth, but will be opposed by those who are filled with darkness and ignorance.

As a light on a tower so shall glow the Diamond of Shambala. One stone on his ring will be worth more than all of the treasures of the world. Even those who help advance the Teachings of Shambala by mere accident will be rewarded a hundred fold. Only a few more years shall pass before everyone will become aware of the mighty steps of the Lord of the New Era.

Already one can perceive unusual manifestations and find himself confronted with unusual people.

Already ripened fruits are beginning to fall from the trees. And the Banner of Shambala shall eventually encircle the central lands of the Blessed One.

Those who accept him shall rejoice.

Those who deny him shall tremble.

The deniers shall be given over to justice and then be forgotten.

And all the Warriors shall march under the Banner of the Maitreya

The Tibetans also had prophecies that their form of Buddhism would end after the thirteenth Dalai Lama was dethroned. This prophecy certainly was fulfilled when the Chinese Communists took control of Tibet and brutally annihilated thousands of its monk-citizens.

The Tibetans and the other peoples living in the heart of Asia have numerous traditions that in a strange way point toward a total world upheaval in our time. For instance, during the long winter evenings, they talk about the mysterious and mystical tradition of Arghati and its ruler, the King of the World. He is believed to be the absolute ruler of an inner world that exists deep under the high mountains of Central Asia. Access to it is believed to be possible only through a series of huge caverns, the entrances of which are kept secret by the local people. Even today many Asians believe that this underground Shangri-la exists deep beneath the earth. Tradition retains some of the prophecies of Arghati's King of the World, made hundreds of years ago, and many Tibetans believe that his major prophecy will find its fulfillment in the latter part of the twentieth century:

> Men will increasingly neglect their souls. . . . The greatest corruption will reign on earth. Men will become like bloodthirsty animals, thirsting for the blood of their brother. The crescent will become obscured and its followers will descend into lies and perpetual warfare. . . . The crowns of kings will fall. . . . There will be a terrible war between all the earth's people. . . . entire nations will die . . . hunger . . . crimes unknown to law . . . formerly unthinkable to the world. . . . The persecuted will demand the attention of the whole world . . . the ancient roads will be filled with multitudes going from one place to another . . . the greatest and most beautiful cities will perish by fire. . . . Families will be dispersed. . . . Faith and love will disappear. The world will be emptied. Within fifty years there will be only three great nations. Then, within fifty years there will be eighteen years of war and cataclysms. . . . Then the peoples of Arghati will leave their subterranean caverns and will appear on the surface of the earth.

The Hindus, too, pass on a similar tradition and wait with great anticipation for the coming of their new Avatar, or World Redeemer. They refer to him as Kalki, and they regard him as the ninth and last reincarnation of Vishnu, their god of peace; but he will force his rule with the sword.

Of all the fearsome incarnations of the god Visnhu, Kalki will be the most awesome and earthshaking. He will first appear coming from the West, sitting on a great white horse, dominating a whole quadrant of the sky. He will be immense, thousands of meters tall, and will destroy all who oppose him. In the beginning, he will be like the Four Horsemen of Revelations, a messenger, proclaiming the end of the Age. But soon thereafter he will begin to destroy and enslave all who have not followed his teachings, vindicating and rewarding the faithful. In the eyes of Hinduism he will be omnipotent and will consolidate his position by destroying the forces of evil. With this cycle of death and rebirth, the New Age of Kalki will commence and it will last forever.

Even from the ancient Greeks come predictions of a worldwide cataclysm marking the end of a great civilization. A calculation made by Heraclitus of Ephesus, a Greek philosopher of the Ionian school, can be interpreted as a forecast of a major world catastrophe. The Greek ideas concerning the destiny of this world—that there would be a period of destruction of the world by fire and flood—were greatly influenced by the views of Plato and other philosophers. Heraclitus who lived before Plato and was, of course, not influenced by him, had come to the conclusion that the world would be destroyed again after 10,800 years, and as starting point for his calculations he took the year when the world suffered almost total destruction. Taking his calculated prophecy and using Plato's account of the sinking of Atlantis (nine thousand years before his time) as starting date, we find that the date Heraclitus set for the end of the world comes dangerously close to the end of the second millennium after Christ.

The Rise of the Last World Leader

Djojobojo, a twelfth-century Indonesian king and spiritual leader, also recorded some of his expectations for the future, many of which have been fulfilled with an accuracy seldom equaled by other seers. He predicted, for example, that a few hundred years after his reign the islands would be conquered by a foreign race of blond, blue-eyed men who would remain and govern the islands for at least 350 years. The men who fulfilled the visionary's forecast were the Dutch who took the islands in 1610 and remained until 1942 when war interfered with their colonialist occupation.

But Djojobojo went a step further when he predicted that the "strange white race" would in turn be driven off by men of a yellow-skinned almond-eyed race of small stature, who would come from another group of islands located to the northwest of Indonesia and would not remain in Indonesia for a long time. Again he was proven right, for such men did conquer the islands in 1942, and the Japanese remained until their surrender to the Allies in 1945. After the Japanese left the islands, Indonesia demanded total independence from the Dutch, and eventually won their freedom after a rebellious struggle.

Djojobojo's vision had shown him that after the departure of the short invaders, brother would fight brother, and racial unrest would tear the new country asunder. The sharp clashes between the Ambonese and the Indonesian government, between the Molukkers and Sukarno's army, fulfilled this ancient prediction.

But Djojobojo also predicted the final peaceful outcome of the conflict: "Soon after the bloody division in the land, a great Spiritual King will come from the West and become the Unifier for a fractured world." By the end of 1983, the "fractured world" of Indonesia had been restored to comparative tranquility, and the fight of brother against brother had ceased. Only the appearance of the Man of Peace remains to fulfill Djojobojo's prophecy.

A slightly different version of the coming of the Man of Peace comes from the Zoastrian Vestas of Iran, who believe that the time allotted for the existence of this world is twelve thousand years. One of their greatest spiritual leaders, Zarathustra, arrived in their midst around the ninth millennium, but their faith in future guidance does not end with him. They believe that his message will be proclaimed again by another like him toward the end of the twelfth millennium, and that he will act as the catalyst to unite the world's religions.

The twelve thousand-year period has little meaning until we deduct the nine thousand years that elapsed between the beginning of the first millennium and the appearance of Zarathustra. Of the remaining three thousand years, one thousand will take us to the beginning of our Christian era, while sometime toward the end of the last two thousand years—A.D. 2000, to be exact—Saoshyant, the Man of Peace, is to appear. Many Muslims claim that this may be Madhi, their long-awaited reincarnation of the Prophet Muhammad. A unifying force, the twelfth Iman is expected to make his reappearance around the end of this century after a thousand years of occultation.

Ever since the beginning of biblical times, humanity has looked forward to the coming of a Saviour, the Son of God, who would reintroduce holiness to a sinful human race and save us all from the influence of a fallen angel. With the birth of Jesus of Nazareth almost two thousand years ago, many became convinced that the long-expected Saviour had come; yet the Jewish nation among whom he was born did not accept him. Until this day they are still expecting their messiah to save the Kingdom of Israel.

Those who did believe in Jesus set out to transform the world, using the principles for which he stood. He prophesied that he would return in the last days of this world's history, a period of unprecedented turmoil, borne by the clouds of heaven. He would judge the living and the dead and end the cosmic battle between Him and Satan.

To many Christians, the idea that a Muslim might be the long-awaited savior of the world seems incredible. Yet, in addition to Muhammad, two other religious leaders have made the same forecast.

In the sixteenth century, the French Cardinal La Rogue stated bluntly that "A regeneration of the Faith will appear in Asia through a descendant of Mohammed." And Emperor Leo VI, the philosopher (886–911), predicted that "in the distant future there will arrive an imperial deliverer, who will save the kingdom and the people. He shall come from the Ishmaelites (Arabs), and will appear to be as poor as a beggar, yet needing nothing. He will be accompanied by two angels. . . . When he makes his appearance to the world, a voice from the spirit world will say to the people, 'Does he please you?' and all mankind will worship him in adoration and he will rule over them."

During the Middle Ages anything that smacked of the supernatural was regarded by many as witchcraft. It is amazing, therefore, that the prophecies of Saint Malachy, an Irish monk who eventually became the archbishop of Armagh, escaped the attention of the witch-hunters.

Saint Malachy was born in the city of Armagh, Northern Ireland, in about 1094. After serving the Catholic church in various functions, he became archbishop in 1129. Highly controversial because of his attempts to initiate social and religious reforms, he finally left Armagh and accepted an invitation to attend the Lateran Council under Pope Innocent II in 1139.

During this trip to Rome Malachy became inspired to write his *Prophetia de Futuris Ponificibus Romanis,* his prophecies concerning the succession of popes who would occupy the Chair of Saint Peter, starting with Celestine II in 1143. In short Latin phrases, he described the characteristics and origins of all the popes who would rule the Catholic church from that moment on.

The mysterious prophecies of Saint Malachy were not published during his lifetime but were presented to Pope Innocent II so that he could read them as a consolation during times of spiritual distress. Shortly after receiving them, Innocent II had them placed in the Vatican Library, where they were rediscovered in 1595. They were included in a work entitled *Lignum Vitae*, written by Arnold Wion, a Belgian Benedictine monk, who introduced Malachy's notes with this casual remark: "Malachy is said to have written some treatises none of which I have come across except a prophecy concerning the sovereign pontiffs. As it is short, and, as far as I know, has never yet been printed, and because many desire to see it, I insert it here."

Saint Malachy's prophecies of the future were hidden in this roster of future popes, starting from his time, the first half of the twelfth century, and extending into what seems to be the present. He describes a pontiff who can be no one else but Pope Pius XI. After him, Malachy sees only six more popes. Then "Peter the Roman" will become the ruler of the church. During his reign, according to St. Malachy, the "City of the Seven Hills" will be destroyed and the "Awful Judge" will try his people.

Since their discovery, the notes have been studied by many popes, and it has been suggested that this material had a direct bearing on the vision experienced by Pope Pius X in 1909, when, while holding an audience, he suddenly fell into a trance. After regaining consciousness he was awestruck by what had been revealed to him. "What I see is terrifying," he whispered. "Will it be myself . . . or my successor? The pope will quit Rome, and after leaving the Vatican he will have to walk over the dead bodies of his priests."

The Rise of the Last World Leader

We don't know whether the various traditions of the coming of a Man of Peace originated in the Far East and came to the Americas with the explorers who began to traverse the American continent as far back as 2000 B.C. Considering the supernatural origin of some of them, however, the idea that they were not necessarily left here by the explorers but were actually supernaturally transmitted to psychic mediums on the American continent, is not an unreasonable assumption. The spirit of inspiration, no matter its source, has never been limited by geographic boundaries.

Montezuma, the proud emperor and priest of the Aztecs, experienced a vision in 1519 before his pagan empire was brutally destroyed by Cortez and his men. He fell into a trance shortly before his death and eventually entrusted the details of his vision to his daughter.

According to her, Montezuma's guiding spirit informed him that his nation would be ravaged by a strange people and that these conquerers would come led by priests and carrying a cross. He was told that the persecution to be carried out by these priests would be far worse than any atrocities committed by any of his own Aztecs, but that this would not last forever. A time period of eight "cycles" would be allotted to the strangers, after which another great change would come over the land. During the ninth cycle the priests would lose their power, but the cross would remain in the land. A Man of Peace would then arrive from the East, bringing freedom and a new religion that would unite all.

Without the specific time element attached to it, this prophecy could be applied at any time in Latin America now that the influence of the Catholic church is on the decline. Montezuma's spiritual contact, however, *did* specify when this change would come about. In the chronology of the Aztecs each "cycle" was the equivalent of fifty-two years. The first cycle began in 1519; the eighth one ended in 1967. The next and last cycle is to end in A.D. 2009, bringing us close to the end of the first half of the fifty-two years reserved for the appearance of the man from the East. Current political and religious developments in Central and South America most assuredly point in the direction of a waning of the influence of the priests of the cross.

The same spirit of inspiration that worked on Montezuma was probably also responsible for the North American Indians' many traditions involving the Man of Peace. A long time before Europeans ever set foot in the Americas, the Hopi Indians of the Southwest already had traditions based on psychic visions that someday there would arrive white-skinned intruders in their lands and that their cruelty would become legendary. But the "nations of ancient knowledge" (countries in the Middle East?) would somehow defeat the Europeans' evil influence over the Indians, and after that, help would come to the Hopis from the East in the form of the True White Brother. This savior will be recognized by his red cloak and red hat and will bring with him sacred tablets identical to those used by the Hopi shamans.

Accompanied by his two helpers—one displaying the Hindu swastika and a cross and the other carrying the sign of the sun—the True White Brother will purify the earth and make it safe. The traditions of the Oglala Sioux also speak of the coming of a Saviour of the Nation who will come from the East, and even though he will look somewhat like the True White Brother, he will be distinguished by his flowing beard and long white hair.

In the traditions of tribal peoples such as the American Indians the forecasts are often veiled in symbolism that has meaning only to members of the tribe. The Iroquois Indians in Ontario, Canada, for example, still talk about the prediction given them by their shaman Deganawida before the arrival of the first Europeans. According to him, the Iroquois nation would undergo a time of great suffering caused by a Great White Snake who would come to befriend them but would eventually turn on the Indian nation and try to destroy them from within. Deganawida foresaw that the power of the Great White Snake would continue until the coming of the Great Red Serpent. At that point all the Indian tribes would flee into the hills to await the final outcome of the battle of the two serpents.

He sees the conflict as one of the most terrifying ever, with the heat of battle causing the mountains to split open and the waters in the rivers to boil:

> There will be regions where all grass will die and no leaves will be left on the trees. Death and destruction will be so horrendous that even both serpents will be sickened by the stench of death. There will be no victor until a Great Black Serpent will join the fierce battle and will make the Great White Snake become victorious after which the Age of Peace will start.

In the end Deganawida saw a great light coming to his people from an easterly direction, and as it approached it revealed its true form—a Man of Hope who will remake the world.

In probing the past for evidences of supernatural guidance in world affairs, one can even find its marks in the time period surrounding the birth of the United States. A story that recalls one such incident first appeared quite vividly in the *National Tribune* of December 1880. And it will have to be included here because of its relevance. Reprinted in the *Stars and Stripes* issue of December 21, 1950, it is a stirring account of a vision revealed to George Washington concerning the future development of the United States, and the end of time. While many critics would prefer to relegate the story to the realms of fantasy, others, believing that the birth of the United States and its historical development was in direct fulfillment of biblical prophecy, see in it a warning for the future.

"The last time I ever saw Anthony Sherman was on the fourth of July, 1859, in Independence Square," writes Wesley Bradshaw, publisher of the *National Tribune*. "He was then ninety-nine years old, and becoming very feeble. But though so old, his dimming eyes rekindled as he gazed upon Independence Hall, which he had come to visit once more.

"'Let's go into the hall,' he said, 'I want to tell you of an incidence in Washington's life—one which no one alive knows of but myself; and if you live, you will before long see it verified. *Mark the prediction, you will see it verified.*'"

This is Sherman's tale as Bradshaw recorded it:

> From the opening of the Revolution we experienced all phases of fortune, now good and now ill, one time victorious and another conquered. The darkest period we had, I think, was when Washington, after several reverses, retreated to Valley Forge, where he resolved to pass the winter of 1777.
>
> Ah, I have often seen the tears coursing down our dear commander's care-worn cheeks, as he would be conversing with a confidential officer about the condition of his poor soldiers. You have doubtless heard the story of Washington going to the thicket to pray. Well, it was not only true, but he used to pray in secret for aid and comfort.
>
> One day, I remember it well, the chilly winds whispered through the leafless trees, though the

The Rise of the Last World Leader

sky was cloudless and the sun shone brightly. He remained in his quarters nearly all the afternoon, alone. When he came out I noticed that his face was a shade paler than usual, and there seemed to be something on his mind of more than ordinary importance. Returning just after dusk, he dispatched an orderly to the quarters of an officer, who was presently in attendance. After a preliminary conversation of about half an hour, Washington, gazing upon his companion with that strange look of dignity which he alone could command, said to the latter, "I do not know whether it is owing to the anxiety of my mind, or what, but this afternoon, as I was sitting at this table engaged in preparing a dispatch, something in the apartment seemed to disturb me. Looking up, I beheld standing opposite me a singularly beautiful being. So astonished was I, for I had given strict orders not to be disturbed, that it was some moments before I found language to inquire the cause of the visit. A second, a third, and even a fourth time did I repeat the question, but received no answer from my mysterious visitor except a slight raising of the eyes.

"By this time I felt strange sensations spreading over me. I would have risen but the riveted gaze of the being before me rendered volition impossible. I assayed once more to speak but my tongue had become useless, as if paralyzed. A new influence, mysterious, potent, irresistible, took possession of me. All I could do was to gaze steadily, vacantly at my unknown visitor.

"Gradually the surrounding atmosphere seemed to fill with sensations, and grew luminous. Everything about me seemed to rarify, the mysterious visitor also becoming more airy and yet more distinct to my eyes than before. I began to feel as one dying, or rather to experience the sensations which I have sometimes imagined accompany death. I did not think. I did not reason. I did not move. All were alike impossible. I was only conscious of gazing fixedly, vacantly at my companion.

"Presently I heard a voice saying, 'Son of the Republic, Look and Learn,' while at the same time my visitor extended an arm earthward.

"I now beheld a heavy white vapor at some distance rising fold upon fold. This gradually dissipated, and I looked upon a strange scene. Before me lay, spread out in one vast plain all the countries of the world—Europe, Asia, Africa and America. I saw rolling and tossing between Europe and America the billows of the Atlantic and between Asia and America lay the Pacific. 'Son of the Republic,' said the same mysterious voice as before, 'Look and Learn.'"

"At that moment I beheld a dark shadowy being like an angel, standing or rather floating in mid-air between Europe and America. Dipping water out of the ocean in the hollow of each hand, he sprinkled some upon America with his right hand, while with his left he cast some over Europe. Immediately a cloud arose from these countries and joined in mid-ocean. For a while it seemed stationary, and then it moved slowly westward until it enveloped America in its murky folds. Sharp flashes of lightning gleamed through it at intervals, and I heard the smothered groans and cries of the American people.

"A second time the angel dipped from the ocean and sprinkled it out as before. The dark cloud was then drawn back to the ocean in whose heaving billows it sank from view.

"A third time I heard the mysterious voice saying, 'Son of the Republic, Look and Learn.' I cast my eyes upon America and beheld villages and towns and cities springing up one after another until the whole land from the Atlantic to the Pacific was dotted with them. Again I heard the mysterious voice saying, 'Son of the Republic, the end of the century cometh, look and learn.'

"And this time the dark shadowy angel turned his face southward. From Africa I saw an ill-omened spectre approach our land. It flitted slowly and heavily over every town and city of the latter. The inhabitants presently set themselves in battle array against each other. As I continued looking I saw a bright angel on whose brow rested a crown of light on which was traced the word 'Union.' He was bearing the American flag. He placed the flag between the divided nation and said, 'Remember, ye are brethren.'

"Instantly, the inhabitants, casting down their weapons, became friends once more and united around the National Standard.

"Again I heard the mysterious voice saying, 'Son of the Republic, Look and Learn.' At this the dark shadowy angel placed a trumpet to his mouth and blew three distinct blasts; and taking water from the ocean, he sprinkled it upon Europe, Asia and Africa.

"Then my eyes beheld a fearful scene. From each of these continents arose thick black clouds that were soon joined into one. And through this mass there gleamed a dark red light by which I saw hordes of armed men. These men, moving with the cloud, marched by land and sailed by sea to America, which country was enveloped in the volume of the cloud. And I dimly saw these armies devastate the whole country and burn the villages, towns and cities which I had seen springing up.

"As my ears listened to the thundering of the cannon, clashing of swords and the shouts and cries of millions in moral combat, I again heard the mysterious voice saying, 'Son of the Republic, Look and Learn.' When this voice had ceased, the dark shadowy angel placed his trumpet once more to his mouth and blew a long and fearful blast.

"Instantly a light as of a thousand suns shone down from above me and pierced and broke into fragments the dark cloud which enveloped America. At the same moment the angel upon whose head still shown the words 'Union' and who bore our national flag in one hand and a sword in the other, descended from the heavens attended by a legion of white spirits. These immediately joined the inhabitants of America who I perceived were well-nigh overcome but who, immediately taking courage again, closed up their broken ranks and renewed the battle.

"Again, amid the fearful noise of the conflict I heard the mysterious voice saying, 'Son of the Republic, Look and Learn.' As the voice ceased, the shadowy angel for the last time dipped water from the ocean and sprinkled it upon America. Instantly the dark cloud rolled back, together with the armies it had brought, leaving the inhabitants of the land victorious.

"Then once more I beheld the villages, towns and cities springing up where I had seen them before, while the bright angel, planting the azure standard he had brought in the midst of them, cried with a loud voice, 'While the stars remain, and the heavens send down dew upon the earth, so long shall the Union last.' And taking from his brow the crown on which blazoned the word 'Union,' he placed it upon the standard while the people kneeling down said, 'Amen.'

"The scene instantly began to fade and dissolve, and I at last saw nothing but the rising, curling vapor I at first beheld. This also disappeared, and I found myself once more gazing upon the mysterious visitor, who, in the same voice I had heard before, said, 'Son of the Republic, what you have seen is thus interpreted. Three great perils will come upon the Republic. The most fearful for her is the third. But the whole world united shall not prevail against her. Let every child of the Republic learn to live for his God, his land and Union.'"

It was not until several years later, in 1781, that the last battle of the American Revolution was fought. Another two years expired before the final peace treaty with England had been signed. During the second half of the nineteenth century the United States engaged in a needless Civil War, a war that, according to the vision, was to take place toward the "end of the century."

This clearly places the third great peril within the next or twentieth century. The vision of Washington does not indicate the probable causes for the third conflict, but it does have all the implications of a conflict of major proportions, one that will involve fighting on American soil. Neither the first nor the Second World War resulted in battles on American soil, so it is clear that the "most fearful" war will still have to be fought.

George Washington commented after the vision, "When the vision vanished, and I started from my seat [I] felt that I had seen a vision wherein had been shown me the birth, the progress and destiny of the United States."

The vision ended with a victory for the United States, supernaturally wrought with the help of a "legion of white spirits." This is already 1984. Is it perhaps possible that this last battle on U.S. soil will be part of the overall great war that has been predicted for the end of the sixth millenium?

3
Michael and Jeane: Prophets of Doom or Hope?

> I came to say a word and I shall say it now. But if death prevents me, it will be said by Tomorrow, for Tomorrow never leaves a secret in the book of Eternity.
>
> —Kahlil Gibran

It is impossible to discuss end-of-time predictions—whether they be psychic, prophetic, or military—without returning to the predictions of Nostradamus, the great French seer who has baffled mankind ever since he wrote his first quatrains in 1555, and the forecasts of Jeane Dixon, the seer of Washington, D.C., who has often startled the world with her accuracy, especially when dealing with major political and religious developments.

Since Nostradamus began to prophesy, with his rare insight into world affairs, numerous writers have attempted to shed light on his mysterious forecasts. Even though much is known about them now, however, and even though certain quatrains have been put to the scrutinizing test of historical verification, he is still, and will probably always remain, a mystery.

Joseph Goebbels, Hitler's propaganda minister, relied heavily on the words of this ancient seer and found himself rebuffed, ridiculed, and believed, all at the same time. Believing in Nostradamus was politically convenient in Germany during World War II because Adolf Hitler was a strong believer in the powers of the occult. When Goebbels walked into the Führer's office one autumn afternoon preceding the unexpected German attack on Holland and Belgium, he brought with him a stack of Nostradamus material. It did not take much effort on his part to convince his leader that Nostradamus had predicted Hitler's rise to power and that, as far back as the middle 1500s, he had forecast total victory for the Third Reich. No one knows exactly what transpired in the Führer's office that afternoon, but we do know that only a few months later, the German Luftwaffe dropped millions of "Nostradamian leaflets" on the unsuspecting Dutch and Belgians, telling them that resistance to Hitler's advancing armies would be totally useless! I was a teenager in Europe at that time, and I remember the leaflets very well. I also recall the fear they created. The German threat was real, and to read reports that an ancient seer had predicted Hitler's success was frightening indeed, even though it seemed farfetched.

The British followed up by dropping leaflets of their own on which they had printed fabricated Nostradamian prophecies that indicated Hitler's imminent destruction. It was a propaganda phase of the war that nobody won.

Michael and Jeane: Prophets of Doom or Hope?

Studying Nostradamus is a bewildering and perplexing pastime, for both the man and his predictions present a multiplicity of problems. Researchers who scrutinize his four-line poetic predictions usually become more bewildered with each passing line, for Nostradamus clearly had the rare ability to see beyond the veil of time. Although he died more than four hundred years ago, his prophetic judgment and his supernatural grasp of developing history placed him first among equals—a superpsychic among the clairvoyants of the ages.

Michel de Nostredame was born in 1503 in Saint-Remy-de-Provence, France and, although born into a Jewish household, was brought up as a Catholic. Brilliant, witty, and inquisitive, he explored natural science, astronomy, and philosophy and later enrolled at the University of Montpellier. He graduated in 1529 as a doctor of medicine and soon became well known throughout France for his success in treating victims of the plague. An uncommonly high number of his patients actually survived the disease. This was undoubtedly due to his refusal to bleed his patients—a remedy widely used in his day and one that cost many lives.

There are many theories as to exactly how he received his vast foreknowledge of historical events, yet Nostradamus himself never attempted to hide the techniques he used. Interest in astrology was at a peak in his time, and when he published his first collection of predictive poetry, known as *Les Centuries* in 1555, it was generally understood that he received his revelations solely from his observations of the heavens, in much the same way the ancient Assyrian and Babylonian astrologers had practiced their predictive "science."

He never denied that this was indeed one of the methods of divination he used, but he did not rule out other occult practices. We do know that he received many of his visions by gazing into the flat undisturbed surface of a bowl of water that had been placed on a brass tripod, in much the same way a fortune-teller might use a crystal ball. Whether the majority of his visions came to him in these ways or from psychic inspiration, necromancy, tarot cards, or a refined form of witchcraft, we will never know. We may conclude, however, that his hidden source of knowledge yielded much about the future course of history and had the power to influence some major future historical developments. But what that power was or who was behind it Nostradamus never revealed, and chances are that he was indeed ignorant of the identity of the mysterious power that showed him the course of the future.

Nostradamus played a most dangerous game in his day, and he was well aware of it. Not only was his time marked by superstition and belief in astrology, but it was also the era of the Inquisition when millions were burned at the stake or died on the rack because they had been accused of heresy or witchcraft. Occurrences that could not be explained by a gullible or ignorant priest were assumed to be of a dark supernatural origin.

To avoid accusations of this sort, Nostradamus confused the dating and ranking of his predictions purposely and wrote them in a truly bewildering mixture of symbols—Old French, Latin, anagrams and other devices—so as to fool the Inquisitors.

As far as we know, Nostradamus did not leave a key to his predictions with anyone. If he did, it has been lost in the dust of the centuries. The need to interpret his predictions without the aid of a key has led to some curious and widely varied versions of his quatrains. Yet many of them are so close to verified fact that his reputation as Europe's greatest psychic seer has continued undiminished.

Although his first book of predictive verse—each of his books contained one hundred verses—was published in 1555, he began making his first prophecies as far back as

1547. Uttering some predictions that hit home, he attracted the attention of Catherine de Médicis, who invited him to her palace, whereafter Charles IX appointed him physician-in-ordinary. The fame Nostradamus won as a doctor faded after he failed to cure his own family of the plague, but his reputation as a prophet grew to extraordinary dimensions. Nostradamus set out to compose a thousand four-line verses (quatrains), each having a specific prophecy locked within its enigmatic words.

Nostradamus, the "enigma of the centuries," has never been out of vogue, and during the past four hundred years, commentators and interpreters have devoted at least a hundred learned volumes to deciphering and decoding the Nostradamian puzzles. Interpretations often differ, of course. One can work out a logical account or sequential story only if one keeps in mind that the seer worked during the Inquisition. One must also devote sufficient time and energy to piecing together the various discrete predictions that deal with a certain event. No matter what method of interpretation is used, some of his predictions have been fulfilled to an accuracy of somewhere between 86 and 91 percent.

The predictions of Nostradamus dealing with the final armed conflict and the end of the world are truly frightening. Not only does he specify the dimensions of the last great war, but he has also listed names of generals, place names, rivers, and mountains so accurately that we can almost see the menacing hand of Mars looming over the remains of Western civilization.

Let me again emphasize that the prophecies of the great French seer must be seen in the context of the Inquisition if they are to make any sense at all. Then, when one examines his material carefully, one feels sure that Nostradamus actually did predict the end of our world. This ominous forecast really begins with the following prediction:

> The revolution of the great seventh number come,
> It will appear at the time of the great games of death:
> Not far from the great millennial age,
> When the buried will go out from their tombs.
> (X:74)

When one looks at these lines in relation to what is known as the Sabbath millennium theory, the meaning begins to fall into place. This theory maintains that, according to biblical chronology, the world will only endure for a total of seven thousand years, the last thousand to end in a climactic war.

In the Epistle of Barnabas, an early apocryphal work, we find one of the first mentions of the idea of the end of the world. Referring to the Bible text relating to the six days of Creation and the day of rest that followed (Gen. 2:2), Barnabas writes,

> Notice, children, what He means by the words *He completed them in six days.* He means this: in six thousand years the Lord will make an end of all things; for in His reckoning the "day" means a "thousand years" (2 Peter 3:8). Therefore, children, in six days—in the course of six thousand years—all things will be brought to an end. *And He rested on the seventh day.* This is the meaning: when His Son returns, He will put an end to the era of the Lawless One. Then on the seventh day He will properly rest.

Even the mysterious book of Enoch, written at the beginning of our Christian era, touches upon the subject of the world coming to an end:

And I blessed the seventh day, which is the Sabbath, for in it I rested from all My labors. . . .

Then I also established the eighth day. Let the eighth be the first after my work, and let the days be after the fashion of seven thousand [years]. Let there be at the beginning of the eight thousand a time when there is no computation, and no end; neither years, nor months, nor weeks, nor days nor hours.

Biblical chronology gives us roughly two thousand years from the Creation to the Deluge that destroyed all humanity save Noah and the seven members of his family who escaped the sweeping destruction. Another two thousand years brings us to the birth of Christ. Another two thousand years takes us to the end of the sixth millennium. The Sabbath millennium theory is based on this idea and holds that the six days of creation and one day of rest at the end constitute a symbolic representation of six thousand years of life on this planet to be followed by a thousand years of rest.

Both the Epistle of Barnabas and the Book of the Secrets of Enoch point out that Christ is to appear at the end of the six thousand years and that following his appearance there will be a millennium of peace during which Satan will be confined. This period has been identified by many as the "day of rest" and the final thousand years before the beginning of the "eighth day" of Enoch.

Nostradamus must have been well acquainted with the basic Sabbath millennium idea, for the harmony between his predictions of the last days of this world and the aforementioned theory is too great to be the result of mere coincidence.

His X.74 prediction shows this similarity. When he speaks of "The revolution of the great seventh number," he undoubtedly is referring to the seventh millennium after the Creation. When he states that "It will appear at the time of the great games of death," he comes very close to the Book of Revelation's prediction of the seven last plagues that will torture the human race as an adjunct to the final battle, which will ravage the globe, especially when he also refers to it happening at a time "Not far from the great millennial age." Biblical prophecy also foretells a resurrection of the dead at the beginning of the seventh millennium, and here, too, Nostradamus is perfectly in agreement, for his words, "When the buried will go out from their tombs," can signify the resurrection.

Nostradamus was a diligent researcher as well as a psychic, and many of his predictions must have been the result of careful study combined with psychic inspiration or psychic insight. He had a highly inquisitive mind and never seemed willing to settle for a solution to a problem if he had any doubts about the end result of his investigation. It was probably this constant probing that led him to arrive at no less than three different calculations of the beginning of the seventh millennium.

In his preface to *Centuries*, Nostradamus said that his quatrains were in reality "perpetual prophecies, for they extend from now to the year 3797." He arrived at this date by using the calculations for biblical chronology developed by Varro, a historian who lived from 116 to 27 B.C.

According to Varro's calculations there were at least 4,758 years between Adam and the birth of Christ. There is every indication that Nostradamus initially held the view that the world would last for 7,000 years after the year A.D. 1555 when he wrote the preface to his prophecies, and consequently he arrived at 8,555 years. From this he deducted 4,758, the estimate given by Varro, and arrived at A.D. 3797 as the year in which the world would end.

Apparently he was not satisfied with this result, and so his investigations into the "time of the end" continued.

Michael and Jeane: Prophets of Doom or Hope?

Three years later he had greatly modified his original conclusion, leaning toward the concept of the Sabbath millennium. Yet he still took the year 4758 B.C. as the starting year, but instead of adding 7,000 years as he had done previously, he now added only 6,000 years, which made his seventh millennium start at A.D. 1242. He probably had this year in mind when he pointed out that "we are already in the seventh millenniary, which finishes all; we are approaching the eighth, wherein is located the firmament of the eighth sphere. This is the latitudinary dimension, whence the great eternal God will come to complete the revolution."

But Nostradamus was still not satisfied with the results of his calculations, and again he began to evaluate and compare various chronologies of biblical history. Toward the close of his *Epistle to Henri II* he presented still another set of calculations and conclusions, and this set tore a hole in Varro's chronology. His new set of figures put the Creation not at 4758 B.C. but at 4174 B.C. Adding the six thousand years leading to the final seventh millennium to that, he concluded that the year A.D. 1826 would mark the end.

Still he was not convinced at the accuracy of his calculations, and eventually modified his figures again. While we do not know exactly how and why he arrived at his final conclusion, he wrote in X:72,

> The year 1999, seventh month,
> From the sky will come the great King of Terror;
> To resuscitate the great king of Angelmois,
> Around this time Mars will reign for the good
>   cause [good luck?].

In this remarkable quatrain, Nostradamus places the coming of Christ—King of Terror to the unbelievers and the slayer of the wicked—at the end of the present century, or about the year A.D. 2000. His reference to the "great king of

43

Angelmois" who will be brought back to life is very probably a reference to a direct involvement of the Mongols in the last great battle, for Angelmois is a near perfect anagram for Mongolois. Again this all appears to harmonize with prophecies found in Revelation where the Battle of Armageddon is listed as the sixth of the seven last plagues: "And the sixth angel poured out his vial upon the river Euphrates; and the water thereof was dried up that the way of the kings of the east might be prepared" (Rev. 16:12).

To Nostradamus, the "kings of the east" were the Mongols who had threatened the safety of Europe during their conquest of Asia under Genghis Khan. The prediction of Nostradamus included the rise of the Mongol armies to become active participants in the last Battle of Armageddon.

Interestingly, Jeane Dixon, the Washington psychic, has forecast the coming of the Antichrist, and furthermore, she states that he will become "aware of his mission in life in or around 1973–74." Even though no one has received any further revelations on him (for more details on this Child of the East see Chapter 5), his persuasive influence is to start in 1973 and end around the time of Armageddon.

Nostradamus, too, commented on the Antichrist: "The third Antichrist, soon annihilated, But the bloody war will last twenty-seven years." If this "bloody war" indeed ends with the annihilation of the "third Antichrist," we will have to deduct twenty-seven years from the year A.D. 2000. Then we will arrive at Jeane Dixon's 1973 as the beginning of the end.

Nostradamus provided another quatrain that zeros in on the end of time, again pointing without hesitation to the beginning of a new time period:

> The twentieth, the reign of the Moon passed,
> After seven thousand years another will hold its place:

And the Sun will give up its tired days
And then shall my prophecy be finished! (X:48)

This final quatrain is highly significant, for not only do we find another reference to the seven thousand years, but we also find him talking about the passing of the Moon in "the twentieth." Is it possible that he is referring to the twentieth century—in other words, the year 2000? We cannot prove how or from whom Nostradamus received his information, but again his source does reveal a startling similarity between his prophecies and some of those in the biblical book of Revelation.

At that point, in A.D. 2000, Nostradamus's major prediction will come to total fulfillment, and his usefulness to those who believe in psychic prophecies will be brought to an end.

Since the publication of *The True Centuries*, and Nostradamus's warnings about the events that will catapult us into oblivion, many other seers have focused on the same basic theme. None of them, however, has supplied as detailed a vision of humanity's last days as Jeane Dixon has.

In 1965, on an assignment in Washington, D.C., I first heard of Jeane Dixon, a real estate broker who is also a psychic forecaster. I had always been fascinated by the extraordinary, and when Clarence Dykman, the publications manager of Ford Motor Company, introduced me to Jeane Dixon and I came away with a first-rate magazine feature, I had no idea that meeting would have far-reaching consequences.

Yet it did, for less than four years later she and I embarked on an intensive four-month collaboration on my first best-seller about psychic phenomena, *Jeane Dixon—My Life & Prophecies*, the forerunner of many other books in the same general area.

It did more than just that, however. Because of a major vision that she related to me, Jeane Dixon has become extremely controversial in the area of psychic predictions of last days events. She experienced a revelation early on the morning of February 5, 1962, that may have foretold one of the most dramatic events in the final moments of this world's history.

We were sitting in Mrs. Dixon's austere dining room in her row house on Nineteenth Street in Washington during one of our first interviews when she began to tell the story of her most memorable vision.

"It began on February 2, 1962, early in the morning," Jeane recalled, "when I was still meditating in my bedroom. Suddenly I noticed the lights in my room grow dim and looking up I noticed all five bulbs of the chandelier darken—except for a mysterious round ball of brilliant fire which glowed in the center of each.

"It did not last long, and when I told my husband Jimmy about it later on that day, he suggested that it had probably been due to a short power failure. Yet the same thing happened the next night—again during my period of meditation. It was almost too much of a coincidence. But when it happened again on the third evening I knew that something of tremendous importance would be revealed to me."

The awaited vision finally came on the next morning when Jeane was standing at her bedroom window overlooking the slow-moving traffic on Nineteenth Street. Suddenly the street scene faded out of view, and her eyes focused on an endless desert scene, broiled by a relentless sun. Glowing like an enormous ball of fire, the sun had cracked the horizon, emitting brilliant rays of scintillating light that seemed to attract the earth like a magic wand.

Within moments after she first looked at the sun, the rays parted, opening up the way for the appearance of a majestic Queen Nefertiti and her husband, the heretic pharaoh Ikhnaton. Tightly holding hands they emerged from the sun's rays, becoming more clearly visible with each step.

"My eyes were drawn to Nefertiti and a child that she was tenderly cradling in her arms," Jeane said softly. "It seemed to be a newborn babe, wrapped in soiled, ragged swaddling clothes, in stark contrast to the magnificently arrayed royal couple.

"It was strangely quiet, and not a sound broke the mysterious spell as they carried the child forward. Suddenly I became aware of a multitude of people that had appeared between the child and me. It seemed," she continued, "as though the entire world was watching the royal couple. Fascinated by the scene that played in front of me, I saw Nefertiti hand the child over to the people—and at that very moment rays of brilliant sunlight burst forth from the little infant, carefully blending themselves with the brightness of the sun, blotting out everything but him."

Jeane closed her eyes and waited a minute or so before continuing. Then she went on in her soft voice: "Ikhnaton disappeared from the scene, but Nefertiti remained. I saw her walking away from the child and from the people, moving back into the dim past, into the secret realm of the ancients. Thirsty and tired, she rested beside a water jug, but just as she cupped her hands to drink, a sudden thrust of a dagger in her bent-over back ended her life.

"I still remember her death cry," Jeane recalled, clenching her hands tightly. "It was awful, piercing and mournful—and when she finally died, the agonizing screams died out with her."

It took many sessions with Jeane Dixon before the entire story came into focus, for even though she had told it many times since the vision had appeared to her, she seemed to remember more each time, and with every successive interview new details emerged.

"My eyes focused once more on the baby," she related during another session. "By now he had grown to manhood, and a small cross that had formed above his head enlarged and expanded until it covered the earth in all directions. At the same time, suffering people of all races knelt in worshipful adoration to the child, lifting their arms and offering their hearts to him. For a moment I felt as if I were one of them. But the vibrations that emanated from him were not those of God. I knew within my heart that this revelation was to signify the beginning of wisdom, but I wasn't sure whose wisdom I was feeling or for whom it was intended.

"I began to sense an overpowering feeling of love, yet the look I had seen in the man when he was still a baby—the look of serenity and knowledge—made me realize that here was something that God allowed me to see without my becoming a part of it.

"I glanced at the clock on the bedside table. It was seven-seventeen in the morning, but even though it was still early, I suddenly felt as if I had just passed through eons of time."

After Jeane related the vision as well as her memory would allow, I asked her about its significance.

"I am convinced," she pointed out, "that my revelation of the Child of the East indicates that a child who was born somewhere in the Middle East, shortly after seven o'clock on the morning of February 5, 1962, will truly revolutionize the world. He will be a direct descendant of the heretical pharaoh Ikhnaton and his beautiful queen Nefertiti, and I have no doubt that he will merge the multitude of believers into one all-embracing religion. I see him form a new 'Christianity,' based on the power he inherited from his creator, yet ultimately he will lead humanity in a direction far removed from the teachings of Christ."

Daniel Logan, in *The Reluctant Prophet*, also referred to the Child of the East. A well-known psychic, Logan bases his statements on his supernatural inspiration.

Asked whether the world could indeed expect the arrival of a new "savior," he answered, "To some extent, it is true. A child who will be a great leader was indeed born in Egypt in 1962. But his arrival will not be the second coming. Nonetheless, he will lead many to recognize the truth. We are working to protect him from the horror that will soon arise in the Middle East.

He regards it as meaningful that the Child of the East was born in Egypt, and he offers a reason for that geographical circumstance, a reason not mentioned by the other psychics except Edgar Cayce: "This [birth in Egypt] is not without significance, as the ancient teachings of Egypt will become known and will be practiced when a giant vault, now buried in the sands of that country, is uncovered. The vault contains books on the teachings of the ancients, and these teachings will be applied to your time. These writings will become a guide for the man of the future. They were meant to be such."

Many astrologers and astronomers see great significance in the date February 5, 1962. They tie the birth of the Child of the East in 1962 in with a significant grouping of planets.

The astronomer Johannes Kepler believed as far back as 1603 that a conjunction between the planets Jupiter and Saturn created the spectacular phenomenon known as the star of the East, which the three Magi saw and followed at the time of the birth of Jesus. Interesting is that a similar conjunction—Jupiter, Venus, the Moon, the Sun, Saturn, Mars, and Jupiter—clustered again on February 5, 1962, this time around the sign of Aquarius. This event has become known as the great Aquarian eclipse conjunction. Its most noteworthy feature is that the two most important planets in this configuration were again Jupiter and Saturn.

Was it mere coincidence that another conjunction between the same two planets took place at the time the new so-called "savior of the world" was born? Or is it perhaps possible that the date for the birth of the Child of the East,

February 5, was supernaturally determined to coincide with a celestial phenomenon that would point toward another similarity with the birth of Christ?

That the vision centered on Ikhnaton and Nefertiti is also significant, for Ikhnaton was the young heretical king who attempted to overthrow the polytheistic religion of the ancient Egyptians and introduce a belief in one god instead. His deity was the sun god, and his new faith was so much against the traditional religious beliefs of the Egyptian priesthood that it caused conflict throughout the country. Jealousy, hatred, and governmental apathy had reached a climax by the time Ikhnaton died and the members of the old priesthood took over once again, destroying the religion of the Antigod, the sun god. How victorious his successor proved to be in eradicating the religion of Aton and returning to the faith of the priests of Amon is shown by the name he took for himself: Tutankhamon.

Brokenhearted, Queen Nefertiti left the central palace and moved into the north palace on the outskirts of Akhetaton. Enraged priests of Amon then destroyed all traces of Atonism, going so far as to demolish the images of the heretic pharaoh.

The pagan Antigod movement based on adoration of the disk of the sun died out until 3,328 years later when, on February 5, 1962, Nefertiti and Ikhnaton again appeared on the scene, this time to present their descendant to the human race.

In her first version of the story of the Child of the East, Jeane Dixon maintained that the little boy would be a reincarnation of Christ. After our many discussions of the significance of the child and the circumstances surrounding his birth and life, however, she became convinced that we were actually dealing with another manifestation of an Antigod movement, this time personified in the form of a child who would become an imitation of the Son of God.

Michael and Jeane: Prophets of Doom or Hope?

Says Jeane, "From what I have seen of this child since his birth, I am convinced that there are too many similarities to the birth and the life of Christ to be mere coincidence. There appeared to be an unnatural planning behind the birth and function of the child. The very fact that the pagan pharaoh Ikhnaton and his wife presented this child to the world seems to indicate that his mission is to continue where their first attempt to deceive humanity failed."

After her later evaluation of the vision, Mrs. Dixon admitted that there was no doubt in her mind that the child is the Antichrist, the one who is to deceive the world in the name of Satan.

By identifying the child as the Antichrist, Jeane Dixon is echoing a prediction made almost eight hundred years ago by Saint Hildegard, a woman who correctly forecast the fall of the Roman Empire, the rise of Protestantism, and the waning influence of the Roman Catholic church.

But Saint Hildegard's vision went far beyond that. Reaching deep into the future, her mind caught glimpses of what she claimed was but a fraction of a major religious development. Seeing a being who would impersonate Christ during the last days of this world's existence, she issued a warning: "He will appear to move in the air, and bring down fire from heaven, produce lightning and thunder and hail, dry up streams, drain the verdure of trees and forests and then restore it. He will also seemingly be able to make men sick or well at will, to exorcise demons, at times even to revive the dead, galvanizing corpses. But that kind of resurrection will never endure beyond a little hour."

These visions of Saint Hildegard show that the details Jeane Dixon supplied about the coming of the Man of Peace are not unique but have been voiced before. It almost seems as if they have been programmed in the collective memory of the human race to be called up as a promise of hope in times of stress.

The similarities between the circumstances surrounding the birth of the Child of the East and the birth of Christ, are in many ways so strong that they cannot be ignored.

The first similarity has to do with the infant's clothing. From the baby Jesus the Child of the East borrowed the swaddling clothes and wrapped his "imitation of Christ" in them before allowing Nefertiti and her royal husband to present him to the world. In Luke 2:10–12, we find the reason: "And the angel said unto them: Fear not: for behold, I bring you tidings of great joy, which shall be to all people. For unto you is born this day in the city of David a Savior, which is Christ the Lord. And this shall be a sign unto you: Ye shall find the babe wrapped in swaddling clothes, lying in a manager."

As Jeane Dixon watched the little child being presented to humanity, she became strongly aware of the compelling force that went out from him. "In his eyes," she recalled, "I found serene wisdom and unlimited knowledge, yet when I 'touched' his 'channel' I felt that his power was not from God."

But the coming of the imitation of Christ was more spectacular than the birth of Christ. All the trappings of royalty were his, and, backed by the disk of the rising sun, he had the symbolic power of a life-giving force that had been put at the disposal of a child who is to lead the world.

The next important similarity between the birth of Christ and that of the Child of the East is that both children move away from their place of birth. For example, an angel of the Lord appeared to Joseph in a dream, "saying, Arise, and take the young child and his mother and flee into Egypt, and be thou there until I bring thee word, for Herod will seek the young child to destroy him" (Matthew 2:13).

After a long evening's interview, Mrs. Dixon finally admitted that she had indeed seen a similar event take place in the child of her vision. "I have seen that he is no longer in the country where he was born, but that he has been taken to another country in the Middle East—I get the distinct impression that it is a densely populated area of the United Arab Republic—by his parents. Why they decided to move I do not know, but I do know that there are strong forces working around him that are protecting him. The possibility exists that the child and his parents may again move to another country."

Her statement that he had moved to a thickly populated area of the United Arab Republic does not necessarily place him in Egypt proper, for at the time she submitted this interpretation of her vision, Egypt had joined with Syria to form the United Arab Republic, and consequently the child might have moved to Syria.

A third similarity exists between Christ's childhood and that of the Child of the East. We do not know much about Christ's life before the beginning of his public ministry, but at the age of twelve, the Bible tells us, he became aware of his mission in life: "And when he was twelve years old, they went up to Jerusalem after the custom of the feast. . . . And he said unto them, How is it that ye sought me? Wist ye not that I must be about my Father's business?" (Luke 2:42–49). During the following eighteen years Christ prepared himself for his three-and-a-half-year ministry on this earth.

Mrs. Dixon explains the strong similarities she sees in the life of the Child of the East: "When the Child [of the East] reaches eleven years of age, close to twelve, something of tremendous importance will happen to him. We will not necessarily begin to hear about him at that time [1973–74], but at this age, he too will become aware of his mission and purpose in life. From that moment on he will expand his influence, and those around him will form a small nucleus of dedicated followers when he reaches the age of nineteen. He will continue working quietly until he is twenty-nine or thirty years, when the forcefulness and the impact of his presence in the world will be experienced. The climax of his mission will last for three and a half years."

In the same way Christ and his disciples spread the gospel, Jean Dixon believes, so the child and his disciples will spread the religion of the false god. The difference will be, however, that they will not stand alone but will have the power and the propaganda machine of the United States backing them, advancing his cause beyond anything we ever thought possible.

"It will be around the time of his emergence," she said, "that the work of the prophet of the Antichrist will have reached its peak." Again the similarity with the Christ story is striking indeed, for Christ, too, had his prophet, John the Baptist, who prepared the way for him. Mrs. Dixon is convinced that as a result of the tremendous propaganda efforts of the prophet of the Antichrist, the influence of Christianity will have considerably diminished by the time the Child of the East is thirty years of age. Christian education in the schools will have come almost to a standstill, she says, and the youth will have become extremely sensitive and vulnerable to the coming of the Man of the East. In fact, she feels that the youth of the entire world will accept him and will work closely with him in placing the world in his eager hands.

Again the similarity with the work of Christ cannot be denied, for in Luke 18:17, Jesus says, "Suffer little children to come unto me, and forbid them not; for such is the kingdom of God. Verily I say unto you, Whosoever shall not receive the kingdom of God as a little child shall in so wise enter therein."

When the Man of the East begins his mission, no one will be able to keep the children from following him, for to capture the youth, and through them the world, the little boy was born.

For a long time Jeane Dixon wavered between her first

interpretation of her vision, which she related to Ruth Montgomery for her book *A Gift of Prophecy,* and the new interpretation derived from having seen the research materials I had compiled on the religious meaning of Pharaoh Ikhnaton's rebellion and other research materials submitted to her by a good friend Father Kavan, a Roman Catholic scholar. But when the true meaning of the coming of the Child of the East finally became clear, Jeane was convinced that the movement surrounding the Man of the East would be totally anti-Christian.

"Like Christ," she said, "The Antichrist will center his work around the city of Jerusalem. I get the distinct feeling that the religions of the Western world will somehow merge with the philosophies of the East. I see the youth flock to him and partake of his wisdom in much the same way that some of them today make pilgrimages to their gurus.

"With the world fully prepared for his coming, millions will be brought into contact with him through our advanced communications networks. The Holy City will become his headquarters, but the world will become his field of battle. Close cooperation between the powers then ruling the United States and this new spiritual ruler will strengthen his contacts with the Americas, and his visits to the North American continent will be frequent and far-reaching."

Not until I returned to Washington for one of our last interviews did Jeane tell me the rest of the story somewhat reluctantly.

She had just returned from an out-of-town speaking engagement when we met at her home and sat down quietly in the dining room. She was obviously tired and in no mood for a grilling on the final phases of the work of the Child of the East. Yet something was missing, and I had a gut feeling that there was more to the story than she had told me. Finally, under consistent probing, Jeane Dixon disclosed the final part of her vision—a rather dramatic and unexpected climax to a vision that already seemed to spell doom for a confused world.

Speaking softly and with her mind's eye searching for the missing details, she recalled the ending. "I saw a great crowd follow him reverently as he walked up a long road," she whispered. "Moving onto this road marked the end of his rule. In awe and filled with blind adoration, they followed him, neglecting to listen to an inner voice that cautioned them against proceeding. I saw him stop and turn around. He gazed at the masses of humanity with a hypnotic look of wisdom and beckoned them to follow him all the way to the end of the road. Once more he turned, and the masses kept pressing on. . . .

"Slowly I saw them all arrive at a fork in the road where the Child of the East slowed down as though engaged in deep thought, and with a gentle flowing of his robes he made a sharp turn to the left. It was obvious that this marked the final point of decision for humanity, for here everyone was given the choice of either following him or continuing on to where the path became straight and narrow. The religious Pied Piper had done his job well, for the overwhelming majority of the pressing throng followed him in quiet adoration.

"I looked over their heads toward the end of the road, and my vision became diffused as I saw the total darkness and utter desolation that awaited them at the end of their journey.

"Then my head turned, and I began to notice the small band of people who had changed their minds at the very last moment and had turned away from the persuasive influence of the Child of the East. They had chosen the narrow road instead and were now climbing across the obstacles that covered the narrow pathway. They had chosen truth, not deceit, and had rejected the Antichrist."

With the vision ended, Jeane's look into the future had reached its limit, but the implications of her supernaturally supplied information were highly thought provoking.

Jeane Dixon's psychic vision shows an extremely close similarity to one of the revelations experienced by Ellen G. White, a nineteenth-century seer who, after a vision she experienced prior to 1850, wrote about a being who, toward the end of the world, would deceive humanity.

"A train of cars was shown me, going with the speed of lightning," she wrote in her book, *Early Writings*. "The angels bade me look carefully. I fixed my eyes upon the train. It seemed that the whole world was on board, that there could not be one left. Said the angel, 'They are binding in bundles ready to burn.' Then he showed me the conductor, who appeared like a stately, fair person, whom all the passengers looked up to and reverenced. I was perplexed and asked my attending angel who it was. He said, 'It is Satan. He is the conductor in the form of an angel of light. He has taken the world captive. They are given over to strong delusions, to believe a lie, that they may be damned. This agent, the next highest in order to him, is the engineer, and other of his agents are employed in different offices as he may need them, and they are all going with lightning speed to perdition.'

"I asked the angel if there were none left. He bade me to look in an opposite direction, and I saw a little company traveling a narrow pathway. They seemed to be firmly united, bound together by the truth, in bundles, or companies.

"Said the angel, 'The third angel is binding, or sealing, them in bundles for the heavenly garner.' This little company looked careworn, as if they had passed through severe trials and conflicts. And it appeared as if the sun had just risen from behind a cloud and shone upon their countenances, causing them to look triumphant, as if their victories were nearly won."

A.D. 2000

Jeane Dixon was perplexed when, during the course of our interviews, I showed her some of the predictions left behind by Ellen G. White, for Jeane, too, recognized the obvious harmony between her vision and that of Ellen White.

Considering that the Child of the East was born on February 5, 1962, and that his grand scheme of deception will be finished around his thirty-third year, one doesn't have to be a mathematician to conclude that we are talking about a climactic event that will occur in 1995, five short years before the close of this century, a time frighteningly close to the calamities predicted for the year A.D. 2000.

The degree of harmony as found in the end-of-time visions of both Nostradamus and Jeane Dixon appears to point to the same source of inspiration—whatever that source may have been.

The announcements of pending doom and the end of the world are becoming more frequent and more detailed the closer we get to the year A.D. 2000. Is it really possible that the prophecies of the ancients are ticking off the countdown to earth's destruction?

4
Storehouse of Anger Spilling Over

> It is only in the most recent, and brief, period of his tenure that man has developed in sufficient numbers and acquired enough power to become one of the most potentially dangerous organisms that the planet has ever hosted.
>
> —G. Tylor Miller

We have now "progressed" to the point where we are beginning to take our own destiny into our trembling hands. We have proudly acquired the ability to self-destruct at the twitch of a neurotic mind. It is a worrisome thought!

In February 1979 in Washington, D.C., James Michener caused some influential heads to bow in thoughtful consideration when he cautioned, "There seem to be great tides which operate in the history of civilization, and nations are prudent if they can estimate the force of those tides, their genesis, and the extent to which they can be utilized. A nation which guesses wrong on all its estimates is apt to be in serious trouble, if not on the brink of decline."

Kenneth J. Holland, editor of *These Times*, reflects, "The common man senses that something unusual has happened, and he fears that he is fast becoming unable to handle life. Students at the University of Maryland, when interviewed, stated that mankind has lost control of things, has lost any leadership it had, and that we are heading for some kind of worldwide catastrophe. A surprisingly large number felt that the next great event facing humanity will be the second coming of Christ!"

Such warnings have been ignored, however. Instead of collective action leading to corrective measures, the politicians of this world have torn down all the caution flags and have submerged themselves in a pool of mutual distrust and cynicism, hoping that it will help them to avoid a cataclysm.

The "ostrich syndrome" is, of course, widespread, but it has not eased our suspicion that nature has been piling up tremendous anger against us. Will it end up destroying us or will we hurry and slip—and end up annihilating ourselves?

> The nations were angry;
> and your wrath has come.
> The time has come for judging the dead
> and for rewarding your servants the prophets
> and your saints and those who reverence your name,
> both small and great—
> *And for destroying those who destroy the earth.*
>
> (Rev. 11:18)

Are we guilty of destroying the earth and should we in turn be destroyed? Have we arrived at that point in history?

A prominent ecologist, Kenneth E. F. Watt of the University of California, gloomily predicts that, at the rate we're going, we could consume and pollute our way to oblivion by the end of the twentieth century. He bases his pessimistic statements on the alarming rapidity with which our modern technological society is consuming the earth's limited natural resources, together with overpopulation, continuous pollution, and the misuse of the environment. He feels that we are consigning our planet and our civilization to extinction.

Watt's prediction is ominous and frightening, but many responsible scientists agree that this is exactly what may happen. Ecologist Barry Commoner, for example, pointed out that we have merely a single decade in which to design fundamental changes in technology if we are to survive. Lee A. Dubridge, addressing a United Nations conference of leading experts on human environment, said that "Our spacecraft called Earth is reaching its capacity." He might just as well have said that man's destructive nature has finally caught up with him, for we have obviously reached the point of no return.

At the turn of the century, the threat of world pollution and the idea that humanity would someday be accused of destroying its own planet and civilization would have been considered absurd. Now, in 1984, it does not seem like such a deranged thought. The human race is running scared—and has every reason to do so.

It is apparent that a person needs more than five smooth stones and a slingshot to face the giant industrial conglomerates that are forcing us to live in a hostile environment where even the air we breathe can kill us. We are confronted with an entirely new challenge—civilized survival—in a world of expanding technology that is rapidly altering our surroundings and exposing us to increased amounts of harmful chemical substances, some of which were nonexistent a decade ago.

This has resulted in what is called the environmental disease. The danger of this disease to the lives of this earth's inhabitants is staggering, for throughout the Western world approximately a thousand new chemicals are produced each year, and more than twelve thousand compounds are already on the U.S. government's toxic substance list. Fifteen hundred of these are suspected of causing tumors, and thirty compounds currently used in Western industries are known to cause cancer. A pervasive industrial chemical called PCB floats invisibly through air and water, and is brought to the dinner table in fish and other foods. It has even been found in mother's milk.

Even Switzerland, once an unspoiled country, is now blighted by polluted lakes. Commented Otto Jaag, one of that nation's leading authorities on water, "Catastrophic deterioration is slowly encroaching on all our lakes. It can be traced to the progressive pollution... caused by dumping household and industrial waste-water into our lakes and rivers." Sometimes, Dr. Jaag explains, even the Lake of Zurich is "turbid and discolored with unpleasant shades of green, yellow, brown, and violet."

Eugene Thomas, a senior chemist of the Zurich Canton reported that often gas bubbles in the lake cause algae "in patches larger than hand size [which are] detached from the bottom so that they float on the surface and form repulsive flat cakes there that look like the skin of a toad."

Industrial "progress" has indeed brought a pollution crisis to the Swiss. To contain or correct the problem, a number of sophisticated water treatment plants have been built to purify the Rhône River before it enters France, and similar steps have been taken for the waters of the Rhine. In fact, the Swiss are so concerned with the problem that they have even paid for the construction of purification plants on the rivers in France and Germany, hoping that the curse of industry can be curtailed. The realization that some of the world's rivers are "too thin to plow but too thick to drink" has scared the Swiss into action.

In the Dutch city of Rotterdam where the largest oil refineries in Western Europe are located, an elaborate early-warning system has been devised to apprise the municipal authorities of fluxes in air quality. Electronic pollution sensors have been placed at strategic locations throughout the area, and when the pollutants become too heavy, computers go into action and pinpoint the source of the offending substances. The authorities have the power to call for a total shutdown of all pollutant-producing industrial activity if that should be deemed necessary. "Our industrial blessing has become our damnation," I was told by an engineer who helped to develop the Rotterdam system. "Why have more and better consumer goods if we won't be able to enjoy them?"

The twentieth-century technology that has generated such affluence in the United States and Europe has also created a pestilence as deadly as the epidemics of the past—although slower acting. "All we have done is exchange bubonic plague for cancer," says William Lijinski of the Frederick Cancer Research Center in Frederick, Maryland.

The implications are frightening. In the United States alone the National Institute for Occupational Safety and Health has estimated that 100,000 deaths from on-the-job pollution occur annually, with 390,000 new cases being reported every year. In fact, the United States has one of the world's highest incidences of cancer associated with pollution—so high that some leading experts conclude that pollution may be responsible for up to 90 percent of all cancers found.

But the result of our purposeful destruction of our civilization will be twofold. Not only are our shortsightedness and blissful ignorance causing an increasing number of deaths, but we are also paving the way for the fulfillment of John the Apostle prediction. We are damaging our planet and its inhabitants at an unprecedented rate, and in doing so we are "destroying the earth."

Jack Shepherd, former senior editor of *Look* magazine, singled out America as a prime example, when he wrote in 1970, "We are fouling our streams, lakes, and marshes. The sea is next. We are burying ourselves under 7 million scrapped cars, 20 million tons of waste paper, 48 billion discarded cans, and 28 billion bottles and jars a year. A million tons of garbage pile up each year. The air we breathe circles the earth forty times a year, and America contributes 140 tons of pollutants."

Recent reports indicate that America's "most productive body of water," the Chesapeake Bay, is dying—and humanity is to blame. Studies conducted by the U.S. Environmental Protection Agency have concluded that the bay is suffering from severe exhaustion and will probably be unable to rejuvenate itself without large infusions of care and money. Seafood harvests have dwindled dramatically. Fish catches are now only 10 percent of what they were in 1960, oysters and crabs are getting scarce, and the rooted aquatic plants are dying.

The big danger to Chesapeake Bay lies in the environmental stresses that are brought to bear on it. With the growth of the cities around the bay and the still increasing industrial development, the fifty rivers that empty into the bay carry such immeasurable quantities of sewage and industrial waste and chemicals and other highly toxic waste products that the waste chokes the bay's ecosystem, slowly killing all life in and around it.

It appears that we have lost all control. Not only are we guilty of polluting the water and air supply on which we thrive, but now we're also exterminating many kinds of plant and animal life faster than they can reproduce. Plankton, the basic food substance of the sea, now blooms a full month later than it did in 1950, motivating one expert to comment, "These changes could have huge and perhaps catastrophic effects on the ecology of the sea if they continue." The possibility that atmospheric contamination caused by our industrial pollutants will diminish the solar energy that reaches the earth from the sun and create another ice age is getting stronger and stronger. Some animal species, once plentiful, are now on the verge of extinction. According to the Smithsonian Institution, the extermination of mammals has increased fifty-five times during the past 150 years, and many remaining species of mammals will disappear within the next thirty years if the killing is not stopped.

A pessimistic view? Not if we consider all the available evidence.

In the last few years some new dangers have been added to our environment—dangers some prefer to ignore, for they are insidious. One of them kills just as quietly and indiscriminately as air pollution but has been unrecognized until lately. Known as acid rain, it is linked to fuel combustion and kills fish, destroys wilderness lake systems, and does much more harm. It does not exact human sacrifices of the magnitude that London experienced in 1952 when its deadly smog killed four thousand people in a terrifying four-day period, but a leading authority on acid rain, Gene E. Likens of Cornell University, regards it as a major threat to the natural life systems. "One has to be very seriously concerned about this kind of environmental insult on the natural systems," Likens has warned. "There is a limit to the stress they can withstand. The forests and the land are the support systems. Without those life support systems to cleanse the air and the water, to provide food for us to eat, our health is just as much in jeopardy as if something is affecting us directly."

Some scientists look upon the reaction of the globe to man-made pollutants as an environmental disaster, for most recent studies have shown that some species of trees, all the way from the mountain peaks of New England to the foothills in the South, are developing dwarfed and deformed. U.S. scientists are now concerned that the problems evident in U.S. forests may be an early warning sign that we will face a catastrophe similar to the one that has already killed millions of acres of timber from Britain to the Soviet Union. The raging sickness can already be found on the crest of the Appalachians, running all the way from Maine to Georgia. Loblolly pine—the staple of the southeastern timber economy—is growing more slowly than ever before. Red spruce now only grows at 74 percent of its 1965 rate. The white pine growth along the Blue Ridge Parkway in Virginia shows a 50 percent reduction in growth rate, while the famed ponderosa pines, which grow on the western slopes of southern California San Bernardino mountains, have already suffered an 80 percent decline in growth rate since the end of the Second World War.

North Carolina State University forest pathologist Robert Bruck is deeply committed to finding the cause of the threatening disaster and has found mountain-crest pollution levels that in many instances exceed those found in the inner cities. In the course of his research he analyzed city rainwater and found that samples of the rainwater found on the streets of Raleigh, North Carolina, have an acidity that approaches or in some cases exceeds that of regular table vinegar.

Acid rain can fall anywhere downwind of urban or industrial pollution, and it now appears to be alarmingly widespread. In some parts of the world a typical rainfall is now about twenty-five times more acidic than *it would have been had the rain contained acid from natural sources.*

According to Lars N. Overein, director of a comprehensive Norwegian study on acid rain, the majority of inland waters have completely lost their fish population as a result of this new pollutant.

Author James Gannon worries about the devastating effects of acid rain in Canada: "Around Sudbury, the acid lakes look pure because they are so clear, but that is an illusion. They are clear because for all practical purposes they are dead! The organic life has been virtually erased—fish, amphibians, invertebrates—all gone. Plankton gone. Algae, bacteria, severely reduced or chemically altered. The entire aquatic ecosystem snuffed out—perhaps irrevocably. When the chain of life is broken like this, the higher animals are also affected. Fish-eating birds and vertebrates have left the lakes. . . . Parts of the barren landscape around Sudbury will resemble what the earth will be like when life is gone entirely."

Fossil fuel in general is a major source of acid, but the recent increase in the use of one fuel in particular—coal—is largely responsible for the heavy increase in nitrogen òxide and sulfur dioxide in the atmosphere. Kenneth Brower commented sharply on it in an article in a 1979 issue of *Omni:* "Scientists of the International Joint Commission predict that, by 1995, fifty thousand lakes in this country and Canada will be biologically dead; widespread destruction of plant and animal life will have occurred; and millions of people will have been contaminated by lead, mercury, aluminum, and cadmium removed by acid from soil, rock, and water pipes."

The curse of pollution knows no national boundaries. The January 9, 1984, issue of *Time* magazine, for example, carried a story called "Turning Green into Yellow," about the fate of Germany's Black Forest: "The dark evergreens that gave the region its name are dying, victims of a blight that is destroying an alarming amount of the forest acreage of heavily industrialized West Germany. In the central state of Hesse, 10 percent of the spruce are now gone; in the northern city-state of Hamburg, almost 25 percent of the pines are suffering. Southern Germany has been hit most severely: more than half the trees in the 2,300-square-mile Black Forest and the 1,800-square-mile Bavarian Forest are damaged, and the devastation is spreading. Last year, according to the Interior Ministry in Bonn, only 8 percent of the nation's forests were affected. This year the figure has leaped to 34 percent. The situation in East German forests is reported to be even worse." In fact, similar reports are surfacing throughout central Europe. In the vicinity of the Soviet auto-manufacturing city of Togliatti, vast stretches of forest land have been turned into desertlike areas. It so alarmed the Russian scientists that even Pravda, which rarely acknowledges pollution problems in the motherland, felt forced to devote considerable space to it. The problem appears to be more threatening since reforestation efforts in Czechoslovakia have failed, and the opinion that the problem might be irreversible is now gaining credence.

The cause? Suspicions focus on environmental pollution, especially the acid rains caused by auto and industrial emissions. West German industries burn 3.5 million tons of coal a year, leading to a heavy discharge of sulfur dioxide. If nothing is done to stop the increasing damage, it could eventually lead to a loss of approximately $11 billion in the timber and related industries. Comments Peter Schutt of the University of Munich, "In my view there is too much talk and too little action. I have no hope at the moment because all the measures have come too late!"

Still another problem has recently been added to our already slim chance of survival. New information released by the Environmental Protection Agency and the National

Academy of Sciences indicates that the earth is warming up from all the carbon dioxide being spilled into the atmosphere by the burning of fossil fuels, and worse, the first effects of the climatic changes can be expected by the 1990s. These fossil fuels, by the way—and there are only 660 billion barrels left unpumped—will be exhausted by the year 2017. We could reach the point of exhaustion even before then if extra energy is needed to solve our environmental problems and growing military needs. The reports also warn that the concentrations of carbon dioxide in the air could double, eventually increasing global temperatures by as much as seven degrees.

Researchers have been cautioning for nearly a century that the burning of fossil fuels (coal, oil, natural gas) is steadily increasing the atmosphere's carbon dioxide content. The invisible gas itself is not dangerous, of course. In fact it is vital to green plants, which combine it with water in the presence of sunlight to produce carbohydrates.

But the reports indicate that there can be too much of a good thing! As the amount of carbon dioxide in the atmosphere increases beyond the capacity of plants or the oceans to reabsorb it, the gas acts as a thermal blanket. Like the glass of a greenhouse, it allows the sun's rays to pass through, but it prevents longer infrared rays, or heat, given off by the earth from radiating back into space.

Gradually as carbon dioxide levels rise, the atmosphere gets warmer. It retains more water vapor, adding still another gas that traps heat. Meanwhile the temperature of the earth's surface rises, melting snow and ice. The water swells the oceans, because of the runoff and the water's heat expansion. At the same time the polar ice caps shrink, and the planet's total reflectivity decreases. The result is that the earth bounces less sunlight back into space and heats up even more. Comments Robert Schiffer, manager of NASA's climate-research program, "It's all straightforward physics."

A.D. 2000

Sometimes it appears that we use innovations without creating adequate safeguards to prevent their possible detrimental effects. The overuse of DDT was an example of this. Manson Valentine, a biologist with the Department of Agriculture in Washington, testified about the deadly qualities of the pesticide. Referring to an experiment conducted in 1948, Dr. Valentine recalled,

> I was on call in the National Museum, Washington, to identify the species of insects, in my case beetles and butterflies, which were exterminated by spraying DDT from planes in a selected test area. The area chosen was a tract of a thousand acres, most of the only virgin forest left in Maryland, along the bank of the Potomac above Chain Bridge. The purpose of the project was to find out what DDT would kill and how long it would take.
> The result was that there was no life left at all. Everything was killed from protozoa to mammals. Everything that flew, climbed, scampered, burrowed, or swam was sent in enormous quantities to a large group of biologists. We had to make long reports on each species, hundreds of species with thousands of members of each.
> It turned out it was fatal to humans, too.... The gardener who worked for a colleague of mine, Dr. Paul Bartsch, a specialist in mollusks, died as a result of the DDT he was using in Dr. Bartsch's garden.
> As I was working on the experiments I began to have "end of the world" thoughts. It occurred to me that if the unrestrained use of DDT were spread it would kill off the animal population and eventually people as well.... Other human fatalities began to occur, and the use of DDT was inter-

rupted in the United States. However, it is still used in Central and South America where entire species of insects, birds, and small animals continue to disappear.

The aftereffects of the spraying of DDT, however, are far from over, and the DDT rate found in Eskimos now stands at between 23 and 25 parts per million, while that of Israelis has reached 19.2 and of Americans 11. What this will do to future generations is anybody's guess—but the eventual results are bound to be detrimental to human development.

In our eagerness to enhance our quality of life we are unthinking about the far-reaching effects our "creature comforts" have on our host planet. Excessive amounts of fluorocarbons used in spray cans of beauty aids, household cleaners, and insecticides combine with the exhaust of supersonic jets as they pass through the protective ozone layer of our atmosphere. We need this ozone layer to protect us from excessive ultraviolet radiation. Any further damage to it could seriously affect both plant and animal life. It has been estimated that the Freon already released into the atmosphere will reduce the ozone shield from 3 to 6 percent. A reduction of the shield by 5 percent is estimated to cause approximately eight thousand new cases of skin cancer a year. If this damage to the ozone layer continues, the increase in ultraviolet could destroy our crops and have a very damaging influence on Earth's agriculture.

What this will do to our rapidly increasing population is still another problem. According to the most recent estimates, the world population now doubles every thirty-seven years. Wars and starvation appear to have little or no influence on human multiplication. In 1830 the world population stood at one billion. It had increased to 2.5 billion by 1950; it was 3.5 billion in 1970 and 4.5 billion in 1980; it should reach 5 billion by 1985 and may climb up to 7 billion by the year 2000. Some demographers have already predicted a population of 20 billion by the year 2100.

The authors of *The Guinness Book of World Records*, the McWhirter brothers, have calculated that, based on the present geometric rate of human population increase, there would be one person for every square yard on earth by the year A.D. 2500. They also figured out that humanity would outweigh the earth by 3700. By 7975, according to the authors, there would be enough human beings to fill all the space in the known universe. Rather farfetched, perhaps, but it does prove a point!

If this is the future for the population of this planet, there will be no way to produce enough food to fulfill the basic needs of the world's people. More than 5 million people starve to death every year, but even this most cruel manner of involuntary population control will not help us avoid the consequences of our growth. The populations of cities of the future will be as large as the populations of countries today. By the year 2000, for example, Calcutta is expected to have a population of close to 70 million, and other major metropolises will also have grown to unmanageable proportions.

While today's botanists are desperately trying to find solutions to the future problems of supplying food to hungry millions, our planet is being transformed into such a densely packed world that it will have the appearance of a gigantic ant colony by the end of this century.

By the year 2000, about 90 percent of the increase in population is expected to have taken place in underdeveloped countries, most of them tropical and many of them rich in plant varieties. Because of the rapidity of population growth, however, fertile fields and wild areas will give way to towns, cities, and mechanized farms, and 40 percent of present-day forestland in developing nations may be irretrievably lost. Much of this area is tropical rain forest where exceptional light, warmth, and moisture foster an astounding variety of flora. One species of plant or animal could disappear from the tropical forests each day, and within a few years the rate could be one per hour, according to wildlife expert, Norman Myers in *The Sinking Ark*.

The seriousness of the danger to animal life on our planet is well understood by the World Wildlife Fund. Organized in 1961 and first chaired by its founder Prince Bernhard of the Netherlands, it is now operated under the watchful eye of Prince Philip, the Duke of Edinburgh. The Fund's aim is to safeguard earth's animal species, and this is the only international organization that champions the animals' right to survival.

A few years ago while on assignment as roving editor for *International Wildlife* magazine, I discussed the problems of wildlife conservation with Prince Bernhard. "Now that so many animals are on the endangered species list," I asked him, "has it become harder for the big game hunter to find unendangered game?"

"Oh, yes, there is no doubt about that," he replied. "By now the number of species in danger has become so large that I tell my friends: 'I will never speak to you again if you shoot one of those endangered animals.' Each year I find one or two new species that are in danger of disappearing and therefore should not even be shot for eating."

I asked him whether the destruction of our natural resources might signal the beginning of the end of life on this planet.

"Well," he replied, "if by sheer thoughtlessness we wipe out a large number of existing species, this means that we are also thoughtless about other things, and the other things are really our own survival. We put our own comfort and materialistic way of life over population needs, land for farming, and other uses."

Right now approximately 20 to 30 percent of the earth's

total land area is still covered by dense forests, but this percentage is rapidly decreasing. Worldwide, forests are being cut down at an annual rate of 1 to 2 percent, which means the destruction of roughly 11 million hectares of forest land each year.

During the thousand years from A.D. 900 to 1900, the forests of Western Europe declined from more than 90 percent of the land to just 18 to 23 percent. Although recent years have brought slight increases in the forestlands of Europe and North America, the developing countries in Africa, Asia, and Latin America are engaged in feverish deforestation. According to estimates based on present rates, forest areas in developing countries will be reduced by about one-fourth by the turn of the century. Already the tropical rain forests are only half as large as they once were, and by the year 2000 only small remnants may exist as a token remembrance of times past.

Frank Don, author of *Earth Changes Ahead*, claims that the most significant example of deforestation is found in Brazil. In the state of Paraná, the forest area in 1953 was 65,000 square kilometers. Over the next ten years deforestation proceeded at the rate of 3 percent a year. With a total land area of 250,000 square kilometers, the state of São Paulo was 60 percent forestland in 1910, but by 1950 this figure had already been reduced to 20 percent.

Latin America is not alone in destroying the forestlands. China is guilty of the same willful destruction. In fact, in one mountainous region in that country the eradication of large forests has been so total that it has resulted in climatic changes in the region. Deforestation is now believed to be responsible for a drop by one-half in the annual rainfall since 1967. In Yunnan province, the loss of 133,000 hectares of dense forest has already led to much hotter weather.

But that's only half the story. Deforestation can cause the spread of deserts as well. In northeastern Brazil, the widespread felling of trees has led to the intrusion of desert-like conditions on a once-humid region. The cutting of timber and overgrazing by settlers have destroyed whole areas of Mexico and the southwestern United States, transforming fertile land into desert. In Australia, continued overgrazing may reduce three-fourths of that continent to desert. The overharvesting of firewood in the Sahel on the southern fringe of the Sahara has accelerated the spread of that enormous desert by some 100 square kilometers southward in the past twenty years.

At present, deserts cover about 43 percent of the surface of the globe, and about 15 percent of the world's people live in these inhospitable surroundings. But humanity continues to violate the earth, and so the deserts keep spreading. It has been estimated that by the turn of the century up to one-third of the earth's presently tillable soil will be lost to the desert. If we wonder and despair today over the suffering caused by malnutrition and famine, we can only imagine the tragedy that will occur when the 20 billion people of the year 2100 make their demands on a much smaller food supply than we produce today.

Botanists are looking ahead and attempting to solve future problems before it is too late. They have devised seed banks where selected seeds are stored to be used during the lean years ahead. But seed banks themselves pose some problems.

The existence of seed banks in no way ensures that plant species will stop disappearing. Scientists do not know, for example, how long and how effectively seeds can be stored in these banks. Some seeds have been known to last for several hundred years, but others cannot be kept fertile for long. And while it is possible to regenerate seeds by planting a few and harvesting the resulting growth, regeneration can alter a plant's genetic makeup. More drawbacks of this storage plan may come to light later on.

Is this what the future holds for us? Will our generation be the one that will destroy the earth and go hungry in the process? Will the sins of our civilization, added to all our other destructive tendencies, tip the scales against us, hasten our ultimate demise, and cause supernatural intervention?

Revelation 11:18 especially the section, "And shouldest destroy them which destroyed the earth," seemed to have no specific relevance to the tide of human affairs until the overwhelming surge of technological development that followed World War II. Only since then has humanity developed the capability to annihilate life on our lush green planet.

Christian scholars often refer to Genesis 1:26, which states that God has given mankind dominion over the earth. The Old Testament scholar, Walter Brueggemann, interprets this to mean that humanity has been given the responsibility for maintaining, ordering, controlling, and safeguarding the earth. "To subdue and have dominion," Breuggemann says, "is not a charter for abuse, but rather a command to order, maintain, protect, and care for."

Brueggemann does not mention a severe observation found in Romans 8:22: "For we know that the whole creation groaneth and travaileth in pain together until now."

A creation groaning? It sounds like an exaggeration, but some scientists now believe that even plants experience pain and distress, just as animals do. When this happens, the plants send out mysterious signals that animals and other plants can receive.

Ever since the birth of this planet, its human occupants have exposed it to their ravaging cruelty. They have always believed that death was an end in itself; they were unaware that the cells experienced aftereffects.

A former employee of the CIA handed us the key for unlocking one of nature's secrets and supplied us with the

Storehouse of Anger Spilling Over

evidence that the rest of creation indeed suffers unbearably at the hands of the human race.

Cleve Backster, a former CIA interrogation expert and president of the Backster School of Lie Detection in San Diego, has increased our awareness of the effects of our destructive actions. In the laboratories of the Backster Research Foundation, he has accumulated an abundance of scientific evidence proving that all creation actually suffers.

In a series of continuous experiments that began in 1966, Cleve Backster has discovered a communications system on an unknown frequency that connects all living things. He has clear evidence that all living cells actually communicate with one another during their moments of distress or disintegration. "Since I have discovered this," he confessed, "an entire new world has opened up to me."

The signals he is referring to are transmitted on an unknown frequency by a cell in distress and are received by every other living cell in the vicinity. The moment something dies—whether a red blood cell, a shrimp, a bacterium, a fertilized egg, a flower, or a plant leaf—the dying cells emit mysterious signals that tell of their death and are in turn received and recognized by other forms of life completely separate from them. Backster has found that a device known as a Wheatstone bridge, when hooked up to a plant—any plant—will receive "agony signals." When the plant is in distress, it invariably activates the recording mechanism and produces signals that very closely resemble those produced by a human being during moments of extreme distress, agony, or even death.

Curious about this phenomenon, I spent some time with Cleve Backster in his research lab.

"Let's sit down in the corner of my office," he suggested, "and we'll connect a plant to my lie detector and then we'll talk. My experiments have indicated that plants also react to human thought and emotions. We should be able to read the plant's reaction on the paper recording tape of the polygraph."

Bob Hensen, Backster's research coordinator, hooked up the plant and we talked. Our discussion dealt mainly with Backster's work for the CIA and my work as a foreign correspondent in many of the same areas where he had worked. We compared notes on various revolutions we had witnessed, and suddenly the plant began to react. A discussion of racial troubles in Washington, D.C., and the accompanying death and destruction in both Washington and Detroit caused the plant to transmit similar reactions.

Bob Hensen interrupted our conversation. "The plant seems to be receiving some sort of danger signals," he called out to us. "It acts as if it's afraid of something!"

Backster looked at his assistant and then turned back to me. A second later he smiled. "Look at your hands, Rene!"

I lifted my hands, quickly glanced at my fingers, and realized that, while we had been talking, I had scraped a piece of loose skin off my right index finger.

"You appear to have killed some live cells," Backster remarked. "Let's repeat it, just for the record."

I located a piece of skin and pulled . . . and brushed away the drop of blood that appeared. The reaction was the same! The plant reacted fiercely, and the tracing it left on the paper strip showed the equivalent of a severe emotional shock.

"We're used to this sort of thing," Cleve continued. "The plants react to destruction of a part of themselves, to destruction of cells of other living things, and to human thought and emotion. Now we are also beginning to realize that cells have a certain degree of memory."

Later on that same day, Cleve hooked up a tone generator to the output section of the Wheatstone bridge and continued his experiments. No longer were the cells' reactions merely recorded in erratic black lines on a strip of slow-moving paper. Now the scratching of the recording pens was accompanied by eerie sounds emanating from a loudspeaker in front of us. Racing up and down the scale, sometimes almost rhythmically, at other moments frantically in a wild profusion of sounds as if emitting one last desperate cry, the cells screamed, communicating their agony to us in a strange unexplainable way.

The idea that "all creation groaneth" is much more than just hyperbole. The sensitivity of plant life and even single animal cells to destruction by chemicals, warfare, starvation, and to the intense suffering experienced by the rest of the plant and animal kingdom, must by now have reached such a crescendo that I am amazed it has taken science this long to recognize the telltale signals.

Can it be that we have finally reached the fulfillment of the prediction made by the seer Daniel (12:4): "Close up and seal the words of the scroll until the time of the end. Many will go here and there to increase knowledge."

Along with other expectations of future troubles that have been voiced for years, forecasts associated with geological changes and disturbances on a grand scale are also gaining more attention. It is as if the very forces of nature are beginning to rebel against the abuse the world has been receiving at the hands of humanity—and have finally decided to retaliate.

For many centuries the human race was totally ignorant of the laws that govern our earth, but now the old misconceptions have been pushed aside to make way for new discoveries. Modern science has destroyed our illusions about a solid and unchangeable earth. We know now that there is no such thing as *terra firma*. We also know that the earth is not a lifeless, rigid, and absolute mass, but has undergone some radical changes and modifications. Entire continents have split apart. Mountains have pushed themselves up from the ocean depths, and great lands have disappeared beneath the seas—and the forces that cause continents to drift apart are still at work today.

Both prophets and the scientists of today are in agreement that momentous changes are in the making and that the earth is beginning to protest in a way we never thought possible. Earthquakes and volcanic eruptions will occur with increasing frequency; in fact, a higher incidence of these events will shake us to the core and will make our survival a constant struggle from now on.

There are approximately five hundred active volcanoes on the globe, and more than one million earth tremors occur each year, of which approximately nineteen are considered major quakes. Two major volcanic/earthquake activity belts girdle the globe, but of course spasms of the earth's crust are not limited to those areas.

Lowell Ponte in his 1976 book *The Cooling* points out that the eruption of Mount Saint Helens may have reawakened at least fifteen other volcanoes in the Pacific Northwest, all of which are part of the so-called Ring of Fire. He feels that Mount Shasta and Lassen Peak in northern California, Mount Baker and Mount Rainier in Washington, and Crater Lake in Oregon are part of that highly active group of fire-spitting mountains that will tear the West Coast of the United States apart as we approach the fateful year A.D. 2000.

The realization that our blue and green globe may actually be shaken by a combination of massive earthquakes, tidal waves, and volcanic eruptions, all happening at the same time, literally tearing our world asunder, is frightening indeed. I vividly recall listening to the tales of the eruption of Krakatoa in 1883 in what is now Indonesia. A force equivalent to approximately 150 megaton H-bombs tore the mountain apart in an explosion that was heard almost three thousand miles away. The eruption and its shock wave created a number of tidal waves, one of which reached a height of 131 feet and destroyed thirty towns and villages. The eruption and tidal wave killed about thirty-six thousand people.

Lowell Ponte described it this way: "Its pillar of ash and smoke, twenty times larger than that of Mount Saint Helens, blotted out the sun and blacked the sky for more than one hundred miles around. For two years thereafter, global temperatures fell by almost one degree Fahrenheit as Krakatoa's smoke shrouded skies around the world."

Other reports tell of ashes that fell on ships sixteen hundred miles away. Shipping lanes filled up with ashes, making navigation impossible. Volcanic dust rose to a height of fifty miles, creating strangely colored sunrises and sunsets. The total amount of energy released in that one gigantic eruption is estimated to have been the equal of two hundred million million kilowatt hours, engulfing the island peoples in a fiery sea of undescribable horror.

Earthquakes coincide with two cycles of the earth's global wobbling, causing a threat of increased earthquake activity every seven years. Such periods are expected to take place in 1985, 1992, and 1999—but more about this global wobble later on in this chapter.

Johann Friede, a thirteenth-century Austrian monk, had a remarkable premonition of the convulsions that will rock the world in years to come: "When the great time will come, in which mankind will face its last, hard trial, it will be foreshadowed by striking changes in nature. The alternation between cold and heat will become more intensive, storms will have more catastrophic effects, earthquakes will destroy greater regions, and the seas will overflow many lowlands. Not all of it will be the result of natural causes, but mankind will penetrate into the bowels of the earth and will reach into the clouds, gambling with its own existence. Before the powers of destruction will succeed in their design, the universe will be thrown into disorder and the age of iron will plunge into nothingness."

While I was interviewing Jeane Dixon for *My Life & Prophecies*, I noted that she often referred to a comet that would strike the earth: "I have seen this happen somewhere around the middle of the 1980s," Mrs. Dixon said, "and earthquakes and tidal waves will befall us as a result of the impact of this heavenly body on our great oceans. It may well be one of the worst disasters of the twentieth century. Although I know the approximate location of the point of impact, I do not feel I should reveal it at this time."

It was a vague prophecy, for without pinpointing the year, the location, or details of the impact, all she really supplied was a hazy hint about a future catastrophe. However, master psychic Nostradamus from whom she may have borrowed the prediction was a great deal more specific on the subject. In quatrain I:69, Nostradamus writes,

> A great spherical mountain about one mile in diameter,
> When peace gives way to war, famine and flooding,
> Will roll end over end, then sink great nations,
> Many of ancient origin; of great age.

The idea of the earth colliding with a comet may not be all that farfetched, even though none appears to be on a collision course with our planet at the moment. A recent report indicates that in 1983 alone twenty-three comets were recorded, according to Brian Marsden, director of the International Astronomical Union's Central Telegram Bureau. Ten of these comets were re-coveries—return appearances of known comets. The orbits of five of the new comets spotted last year keep them relatively close to the sun.

Now, of course, many sky watchers wonder how many more undiscovered comets are still waiting to be found, and whether one of them might just be on a dangerous course.

All ancient seers, including Nostradamus, spoke of the last great war in relation to major geological changes. According to the sequence of events Nostradamus provided for the last part of this century, around the time of a developing war in the Far East, a meteor will plunge into the Indian Ocean with devastating effects, creating tidal waves that will seriously affect the surrounding nations. East Africa, Australia, and Southern Asia will feel the destructive power of this alien giant, adding to the confusion that will already have been generated by the escalating war.

Nostradamus described the meteor as a "great round mountain" and gave its size as "seven stades." The stade was a variable Greek measure equivalent to 607 to 738 feet. Seven stades would make the "round mountain" approximately one mile in diameter. The "mountain" is surely a meteor, for the third line of the quatrain tells us that the "mountain" will "roll end over end" and that in its revolving motion it will "sink great countries."

Nostradamus states that "many of ancient origin; of great age" will experience the wrath of the comet. Several ancient civilizations, of course, were located near the Nile in Egypt, in Mesopotamia, and in the Indus Valley. A glance at the world map reveals that all of these areas border on, or are in close proximity to, the Indian Ocean.

Immanuel Velikovsky, known for his considerable research into the workings of the cosmos, contends that any large body of gases or dust—and this would include a comet—is electrically charged. Thus, each has its own magnetic field. If, therefore, a meteor's magnetic field came into contact with that of the earth, it would result in tremendous friction that in turn would produce a thermal effect on the globe. At that point, a chain reaction would begin, according to Velikovsky. First, the atmospheric temperature would rise. This would lead to an increase in the saturation level. Being able to store more moisture, the atmosphere would not as readily release it in the form of rain as in the past, causing a heating up of both air and water. As a result, the hot air and the warmed water would begin to melt the northern polar ice cap. This would raise the water level of the oceans and would have other equally serious consequences. The Arctic region is a high-pressure area where storms originate and begin their southward movement. A melting ice cap would allow the northern air to absorb more moisture for a longer period of time and would also force the storm patterns to follow a more northerly route than usual, leaving very little or no rain at all for America, Europe, and Asia.

Real problems for the rest of the globe will come when the Antarctic glaciers begin to melt. Remember that the southern glaciers are located on land and are not displacing sea water. Thus, the meltwater from the northern ice cap may increase the ocean's water level by at most a few feet, but when the southern glaciers also melt, the ocean levels may rise by another *three to four hundred feet,* flooding most of the coastal areas of all continents. That the earth's crust will groan under the resulting shift is understandable, and one does not need to be a prophet to expect radical geological changes.

Nothing, however, lasts forever, and after a time, the thermal effects of the impact of the meteor will slowly dissipate. When that happens, world temperatures will gradually return to normal, causing all the stored-up moisture to be released. This moisture will mix with the dust of the meteor's impact, which will still encompass the globe, and a dense cloud layer will form, blocking the rays of the sun and bringing about a drop in the earth's temperatures. Uncontrollable weather conditions like snow, hail, and extremely low temperatures may follow until eventually the atmosphere has dumped all its excess water. Then the world will once again enjoy a reasonable climate—this time, however, amid the total devastation caused by floods, earthquakes, and mud slides.

Not exactly a world such as we enjoy today!

Visionaries have provided us with a great many predictions of major geological changes and earth movements that will affect nations in the years immediately preceding the last world war.

Edgar Cayce, Kentucky's "sleeping seer" (1877–1945), made some of the most astounding predictions of this sort. Cayce said that a forty-year period of geological alterations began in 1958. The early changes, he predicted, would be relatively insignificant, but those that occurred between 1979 and 1998 would be major changes accompanied by great violence and wholesale destruction. For example, he sees the South Pacific as the region where the breakup of the earth's crust will begin.

Nostradamus also zeroed in on the South Pacific, but he described it differently:

> Under the climate opposite to the Babylonians
> There will be a great effusion of blood,
> The unrighteous will be on land and sea, in the air and sky,
> Sects, famine, reals, plagues and confusion [will reign]. (I:55)

Nostradamus probably uses the word "climate" for what he elsewhere calls the "climactic degree"—in other words, the spot on the globe that is opposite ancient Babylon; that would be the South Pacific. He envisions "great effusion of blood," suggesting a major disaster at a time in this century when the "unrighteous" [warriors] will be "in the air and sky"—a clear reference to the use of aircraft in battles of the twentieth century.

In 1941, Edgar Cayce made this prediction: "In the next few years, lands will appear in the Atlantic as well as in the Pacific. And what is the coastline now of many a land will be the bed of the ocean. Even many of the battlefields of the present will be ocean, will be the seas, the bays, the lands over which the new order will carry on their trade with one another."

Other areas likely to experience volcanic activity and earthquakes include the Ring of Fire in the Orient. Cayce declared that Japan is apt to suffer severe destruction in the near future. In fact, he saw the entire Pacific basin shaking to its very foundation, breaking up the land and causing destructive tidal waves to race miles inland.

On the eventual destruction of the European continent, both Cayce and Nostradamus supply us with a virtual treasure trove of psychically obtained information. Both psychics see the first changes in the crust of Europe begin in the vicinity of the Mediterranean. Cayce expects Mount Etna to erupt dramatically, tearing at the earth convulsively. Then heavy tremors will cause the bottom of the Mediterranean to heave up and down in continuous spasms. We already have indications of movement, for seismic soundings in the coastal areas of Greece and Morocco have recorded noticeable elevation changes on the sea bottom.

Nostradamus had been warned by his inspirational sources that earth tremors would take place in specific areas of the Mediterranean. In III:3 and II:52, he left us his warnings:

> In the depths of Asia one will say the earth trembles,
> Corinth, Ephesus then in perplexity.

> For several nights the earth will tremble:
> In the spring two efforts in succession:
> Corinth, Ephesus, will swim in the two seas.

It appears that both psychics tapped the same source of information, for Corinth, in eastern Greece, and Ephesus, in Turkey, are both in the Mediterranean region. Nostradamus also points out the location of the epicenter of this quake that will cause all the "perplexity." His visionary eyes have placed it in the "depths of Asia."

The quake he spoke of will tear the ocean bottom apart and create gigantic fissures underneath the waters. Thousands of miles away from the Mediterranean, two major quakes ("two efforts in succession") will have such a ripple effect that they will shake the coastal areas of Greece and Turkey, and the aftershocks will actually submerge the cities of Corinth on the Ionian Sea and Ephesus on the Aegean.

The intensity of the quake can be seen from still another Nostradamian prediction:

> At the place where Jason had his ship built,
> There will be a flood so great and so unexpected
> That one will have no place or land to fall upon,
> The waves to mount Fiesole, Olympia. (VIII:16)

He was quite specific in this quatrain, mentioning Jason, Fiesole, and Olympia. Going back into classical history and mythology, we find that Jason had his ship built in Iolcus, in northern Greece, not far from Corinth. Nostradamus predicts that the towering flood will reach not only Iolcus but Fiesole and Olympia as well. Mount Olympus is slightly more than 9,570 feet high, which gives us an indication of the enormous size of the tidal wave. In Fiesole (Faesulae) in central Italy, one mountain rises 950 feet above sea level. There is little doubt that Nostradamus actually "saw" the waters rise to that level and that it terrified him, but he also foresaw the destructive deluge not only reaching the populated areas of the Mediterranean but extending far beyond that:

> Great Britain, comprising England
> Will be flooded very high with water.
> At the same time the League of Aausonia [southern Italy] will be at war,
> And striving against their enemies. (III:70)

> When the French will prepare for great evil at the River Po,
> The maritime Lion [Britain] will be in hopeless terror.
> People will flee over the sea in countless number,
> But a quarter of a million will not escape. (II:94)

At the very time that decisive engagements are taking place and the French troops have taken up defensive positions along the River Po against the easterners, England will be inundated to such an extent that its government and its people will be forced to flee the island nation. This desperate attempt to flee will cost the lives of 250,000 Britons, according to Nostradamus.

Nostradamus predicts in no uncertain terms the flooding of Great Britain, but he limits the destruction to the specific area "comprising England"—the southern part of the country.

If we take a close look at the map showing the topographical elevations of Britain, we can see that the land in England is generally lower than that in its neighbor to the north, Scotland. In three other verses, in fact, Nostradamus describes events to take place on the "Island of Scotland."

Storehouse of Anger Spilling Over

Scotland is not a separate island now, but it certainly would become one if England were submerged as a result of a major earth disturbance.

Several other modern and ancient seers have made similar predictions. We have already touched on those of Edgar Cayce, who sees changes taking place in Europe in "a twinkling of an eye" due to geological alterations. John Pendragon, the well-known English psychic who died in 1970, foresaw London partly submerged and the lowlands of his native nation covered with water. Madame Blavatsky, an Asian mystic and psychic, forecast in 1882 that the British Isles would be the first among many nations to suffer from earth upheavals and vast floods.

Malthasar Mass, a seventeenth-century seer, was just as precise in his prediction. In a vision, he saw an island overwhelmed by a deluge and soon swallowed up by an angry sea. Shortly after his vision of this tragedy, Mass claimed to have had a dream in which he saw the waters recede little by little until the upper portions of submerged towers began to appear again. A voice then told him that he was witnessing England reappearing out of the sea.

Nostradamus thought about England often, as another quatrain indicates:

> The great city of the maritime ocean,
> Will be surrounded by a crystalline swamp.
> (IX:48)

Strange wording indeed, but inasmuch as Nostradamus had already identified the "maritime city" with London in II:51, this is clearly another reference to the submersion of that city. Yet the line suggesting that it will be "surrounded by a crystalline swamp" adds a new touch. It seems to indicate that the surrounding area as well as the city of London will be covered by shallow swamplike water. The "crystalline" condition he refers to probably is in reference to the frostlike climate that will prevail on and around Scotland while England is submerged (X:66).

The submersion of England will not be an isolated occurrence but part of an overall pattern of worldwide destruction. This is indicated in another one of the sixteenth-century seer's prophecies:

> The earth will tremble at Mortara [northwestern Italy]
> Tin Saint George [England] half submerged,
> When peace shall be at sleep and war be awakened,
> The temple [Westminster Abbey in London]
> will rip open with great cracks at Easter time.

This verse clearly connects the two events. Southern England was known to the ancient Phoenicians as the Tin Island, and Saint George, is of course, the patron saint of England. Again, England and not all of Britain is specified to be half-submerged. Is it possible that the earthquake in Italy will be a sympathetic reaction to the sudden inundation of a large part of Britain, resulting in a massive shifting of surface weight and pressure?

Many interpreters are mystified by the "temple" mentioned by the master psychic, where he claims great cracks will "rip open" the sanctuary at Easter time. The verse mentions only two possible locations for the temple: Mortara, in Italy, and England. Mortara is easily eliminated, for it has no temple, but England does possess a temple, which Nostradamus referred to twice before. In VIII:53 he mentioned the "Temple of the Sun" situated across the English Channel from Boulogne. The British commentator Charles A. Ward identified this temple as Westminster Abbey in London, built on the former site of a temple to the sun god

Apollo, which was destroyed in A.D. 154. The association between the "temple" and Westminster Abbey is further verified in another verse (VI:22) where Nostradamus talked about a "great heavenly temple" located in London.

The prophecy of Nostradamus states that "The temple will rip open with great cracks at Easter time." A depression in the earth's crust runs along the northern bank of the Thames River. This depression passes beneath the Strand, Fleet Street, and Cornhill in the City of London. If pressure were exerted on this depression, the bed could easily give way and buckle, causing serious ruptures in the earth's surface in much of London, and almost certainly ripping up the floor of Westminster Abbey.

According to Nostradamus, the convulsive earth will be like a wounded animal, its spasms radiating out in all directions, shaking, twitching violently, indiscriminately rocking to and fro, destroying nations, and reducing cities to rubble. New York is one such city and is not overlooked in the visions of Nostradamus:

> Volcanic fire from the center of the earth
> Will cause an earthquake around the new city.
> Two great rocks will oppose one another for a long time.
> Then rivers will turn red. (I:87)

> Garden of the world near the new city
> On the way to the manmade mountains,
> They will also be taken and plunged into the bay,
> Its people forced to drink poisoned stinking water.
>   (X:49)

What better name for New York City than "new city?" What better way to describe the fertile agricultural state next to New York, the Garden State of New Jersey? Nostradamus describes a force of such magnitude that it will topple many of New York's "manmade mountains" (skyscrapers) into New York Harbor, and after the water mains are broken by the quake, only the polluted water of the Hudson and East rivers will be available to quench the parched throats of the few remaining city dwellers.

In predicting the destruction of the new city, the Frenchman was far ahead of present-day psychics who forecast a very similar event. Many twentieth-century psychics agree with Nostradamus that something ominous is indeed brewing within the rocky strata underlying New York City. For example, Criswell has predicted that New York will be totally submerged in the 1980s. He sees earth tremors totally reshaping the East Coast of the United States, with Long Island soon being inundated and Manhattan turning into the "Venice of America"—a city of canals. He is convinced that the submersion of the city will be so total that its inhabitants will eventually be forced to flee to higher ground in order to survive.

From Ireland comes practially the same dire message. The Irish clairvoyant Jim Gavin received almost the same information from his sources regarding the destruction of New York City a few years ago. He predicted that Staten Island would sink like a "raft being pulled under water," and he foresaw lower Manhattan tilting into the bay, the waters reaching as far uptown as Fifty-ninth Street!

Is this possible? Geologists have known for many years that New York is, in fact, not built on very stable ground, even though the ground is very rocky. Commentator Hugh Allen in *Window in Providence* (1943), made a disturbing observation, based on a study by William Hobbs. According to Allen, because of the distribution of the various faults underlying New York, Manhattan Island would, in the event of an earthquake, "break up into three large chunks,

Storehouse of Anger Spilling Over

destroying all the major New York landmarks, as well as seriously affecting its millions of inhabitants."

Actually, the fault lines under New York City are only a small part of a larger earth fracture that begins in Maine and runs beneath parts of Boston and Philadelphia. In the third line of the quatrain quoted above, the French prophet predicted that "two great rocks will oppose one another for a long time." These "two rocks" may be the two lines of rock on either side of the New England fracture zone, which would push against each other during an earthquake.

In 1932, Edgar Cayce may have hinted at the extent of the area that will be affected by all this. He was asked what major earth movements could be expected in America in the near future. While in trance, he replied that alterations would take place in the western, central, and eastern portions of the country, but that the greatest changes of all would occur along the East Coast. Nine years later, in 1941, he specified that New York and Connecticut would be totally reshaped and that New York City would completely disappear beneath the water. He also predicted that land farther to the south—portions of North Carolina, South Carolina, and Georgia—will also be covered by water.

In much the same way, British psychic John Pendragon predicted shortly before his death that all of the Atlantic Coast from Boston to Baltimore will be utterly destroyed. The center of the destruction, according to him, will be New York, but serious reverberations will be felt within a radius of five hundred miles of that city, which would include Pittsburgh and Philadelphia. Nothing, he claimed, will be left of these metropolises except the sunken holes.

Is it possible that we may, through out own hasty actions, trigger some of these disasters?

On September 14, 1978, the Soviet Union carried out an underground thermonuclear test in southern Siberia. The resulting earth tremors may well have been the cause of the earthquake that hit Tabas, Iran, thirty-six hours later, killing twenty-five thousand people. Prominent German and British seismologists believe that it is probable, not merely possible, that the bomb test caused this earthquake.

The destruction in the United States, however, will not be limited to the East Coast. Edgar Cayce said that "Los Angeles, San Francisco—most of these will be among those that will be destroyed before New York even." He even indicated the time when this would occur: "If there are the greater activities in the Vesuvius or Pelée, then the southern Coast of California—and the areas between Salt Lake and the southern portions of Nevada—may expect, within the three months following same, an inundation by the earthquake.

California sits astride the San Andreas Fault, an earth fracture fifteen miles deep and about two thousand miles long, with a pressure that has been building up for years, waiting for an event to occur that will trigger its release. If and when that happens, devastation of the Golden State may be total.

Many seers predict earthquakes and tidal waves for South America, new land rising in the Caribbean, and upheavals in the central region of the United States. Eventually the waters of the Great Lakes will cease to flow into the St. Lawrence River and will instead force their way southward toward the Gulf of Mexico.

This may seem utterly fantastic, yet it all makes sense in light of the theory of plate tectonics, which was proposed by the Canadian geophysicist J. Tuzo Wilson in an article in *Nature* in 1965. Wilson introduced the concept of the "transform fault" and suggested that the earth's surface is broken into several major plates and a number of smaller plates. These plates contain both the continental masses and regions of the ocean floors. The earth's upper layers, according to Wilson, are divided into the asthenosphere and the lithosphere, the latter constituting the earth's crust and part of the upper mantle that has cooled and become rigid. The lithospheric plates ride along the plastic flow of the asthenosphere, the part of the upper mantle where rocks still have a plastic quality.

Wilson claims that plates can behave in three different ways: (1) in accord with sea-floor spreading, plates can be created at the midocean ridges; (2) existing plates can be destroyed at the ocean trenches; and (3) plates can slide past each other causing horizontal tearing or shearing. Faults such as these have been related to the structural geology of New Zealand, Turkey, Japan, and California, along the notorious San Andreas fault.

Since Wilson proposed his ideas, a range of six to nine major plates and about a dozen smaller plates have been defined, estimated to be about a hundred kilometers thick. Since all the plates are naturally interconnected, activity at one point in this crusty mosaic of the surface of the earth's crust can have effects thousands of miles away. It is thought, for example, that the earthquake that destroyed the Chinese city of T'ang-shan in July 1976, killing approximately 750,000 people, may have been caused by the continuing collision between the Indian subcontinent and Eurasia, 2,500 miles away.

The devastation caused by a major quake is so awesome, both materially and psychologically, that even though we know we are unable to contain the forces of nature, we must continue to hope that modern technology will someday be able to predict the time and place of an earthquake.

Four countries are currently engaged in a major research program aimed at developing predictive techniques that could save thousands of lives during future quakes. Teams from Japan, China, the USSR, and the United States are gathering geophysical data in the hope that the accumulated knowledge will minimize the loss of life expected when the major prophecies about New York and the West Coast are fulfilled.

It is ironic that our own senses are so dulled that we have to rely on technology to inform us of the pending movements of nature. Other living creatures don't have that problem. Certain animals behave in a highly abnormal fashion hours, days, and sometimes even weeks before an earthquake. Reports from various countries tell of chickens refusing to roost, cattle panicking in their barns, dogs barking wildly, and rats running dazed into the streets before an earthquake struck. Prior to the Alaskan quake of 1964, Kodiak bears woke up out of their hibernation weeks ahead of schedule and moved into the hills. Even ants react. Russian scientists noted a colony of ants picking up their eggs and embarking on a mass migration. Shrimp were seen crawling out of the water, looking for safety on dry land hours before the quake hit. Many zookeepers have noticed strange and unusual behavior in their animals prior to earthquakes. Tigers, for instance, will stop their pacing. And one panda sat quietly in a corner, held its head, and moaned softly. From the Japanese come reports of catfish leaping out of the water as if to escape something terrifying or moving into rivers where they are normally not found at all. These behavior changes may be caused by fluctuations in the earth's magnetic field.

But one issue is forgotten—perhaps purposely—by psychics and prophets. The scientists, however, are studying it, and the implications of this phenomenon are perhaps more frightening than any of the other dangers we face.

Known as the pole shift, it is a changing of the position of the earth's axis in relation to other heavenly bodies without a change in our orbit. The pole shift could trigger all of the end-of-the-world catastrophes predicted by the psychics and prophets. It can even help us forget about the possibility of a polar meltdown as the result of a meteor crashing into the Indian Ocean.

As Tom Valentine explains in *The Life and Death of Planet Earth*, the pole shift involves a sudden displacement of the earth's crust by a three- to four-mile thick ice mass at the South Pole. This ice mass is so immense that it would reach all the way from Canada to the Gulf of Mexico and from the Atlantic Ocean to the Pacific.

Is there really so much ice on the South Pole that it will present a danger to our civilization within the near future?

Research conducted by Giovinetto and Robinson, quoted in Colin Bull's book *Snow Accumulation in Antarctica*, indicates that between 1966 and 1980 alone, 6,000,000,000,000 tons of ice have been added to the South Pole of our unfortunate planet, greatly increasing the danger that the wobbling effect of our earth will worsen over the next few years.

Commenting on this, Albert Einstein once wrote.

> In a polar region there is continual deposition of ice, which is not symmetrically distributed about the pole. The earth's rotation acts on these unsymmetrically deposited masses, and produces centrifugal momentum that is transmitted to the rigid crust of the earth. The constantly increasing centrifugal momentum produced in this way will, when it has reached a certain point, produce a movement of the earth's crust over the rest of the earth's body, and this will displace the polar regions toward the equator.

What will be the effect when the earth wobble swings our planet off center and causes the polar ice masses to move toward the equator, as Einstein says it could?

In *Ice, the Ultimate Disaster,* Richard W. Noone provides an answer—but it isn't an altogether pleasant one:

> During a pole shift, as trillions of tons of water and ice from the South Pole rush in a wave of destruction thousands of feet high north toward the equator, and as trillions of tons of water and ice from the North Pole sweep toward the equator, the forces of nature, loosed from their equilibrium, will rage wildly in search of a new equilibrium. Volcanoes will erupt, tidal waves will hurl themselves across many lands, global hurricanes of almost unimaginable size will roar around the globe, earthquakes ripping open nuclear plants will create "dead zones," so it will be only the survivors who will be left to worry about climate changes.

When is this to happen? Scientists are cautious about making predictions, and for a theory as seemingly preposterous as this one they make no exceptions! Yet there are indications that polar shifts have taken place before. In fact, Hugh Auchincloss Brown, after fifty years of research, has become convinced that a polar shift happens about once every six thousand years. He believes that Antarctica was still free of ice six thousand years ago. Examination of sediment samples taken from the bottom of the Ross Sea in 1949 during the Byrd Antarctic Expedition have revealed that the last warm period in Antarctica ended about 4000 B.C., or almost six thousand years ago, supporting Hugh A. Brown's conclusions.

Is it possible that the earth is merely getting tired and old and that we are now observing its dying convulsions? Or is the earth taking revenge on its human population for the thousands of years of neglect and willful destruction of its beauty? Or is the earth itself perhaps being manipulated in a mysterious way by supernatural forces in direct fulfillment of prophecy? Is it being used as a means to destroy us?

Biblical prophecy has always been quite direct in its approach to the end of the world. The small percentage of prophecies that remain to be fulfilled are very explicit in describing some of the events leading to the grand finale of this world. And references to earthquakes and possibly even the fiery volcanic eruptions with their thundering noises are often included.

Echoing the words found in Luke 21:11, where counsel is given about the events preceding the end of the world, the seer John gives us these solemn warnings—just to prepare us for some of the happenings of the last days on the planet Earth:

> When he opened the sixth seal, I looked, and behold, there was a great earthquake . . . and every mountain and island was moved from its place. (Rev. 6:12,14)

> . . . and there were peals of thunder, loud noises, flashes of lightning, and an earthquake. (Rev. 8:5)

> And at that hour there was a great earthquake, and a tenth part of the city fell; seven thousand people were killed in the earthquake. (Rev. 11:13)

> And there were flashes of lightning, loud noises, peals of thunder, an earthquake, and heavy hail. (Rev. 11:19)

> And there were flashes of lightning, loud noises, peals of thunder, and a great earthquake such as had never been since men were on earth, so great

was that earthquake. The great city was split into three parts, and the cities of the nations fell. (Rev. 16:18,19)

And every island fled away; and no mountains were to be found. (Rev. 16:20)

5

The Far-Reaching Visions of John of Patmos

> And we have the word of the prophets made more certain, and you will do well to pay attention to it, as to a light shining in a dark place, until the day dawns and the morning star rises in your hearts.
>
> — Saint Peter

In connection with psychic predictions and the words of the ancient prophets, certain questions always come up: Is there really a place for prophets in our enlightened society? And how much faith should we have in the supernatural?

From time immemorial, people have been frightened by the idea that outside forces might be influencing or controlling them. For those who believe in supernatural intervention in human affairs, however, faith in the existence of a higher power is practically inevitable. And whether the critics agree or not, the majority of people regard supernatural phenomena as events to be reckoned with, in both temporal and spiritual affairs.

Throughout the centuries psychic seers and enlightened prophets have announced their forebodings of history, and in so doing have either forecast the future or have in some way affected the development of entire civilizations. Many of these seers have left their legacy to us, but no other single book contains as much authoritative material on the subject as do the prophetic books of the Bible. It is the only prophetic book that contains substantiated history as well as authenticated prophecy. In fact, this compilation of sacred writings is saturated with prophetic utterances: no less than 3,856 texts of the Old Testament are prophetic in nature, and one out of every 28 verses in the New Testament is prophetic!

Since so much of the Bible is prophecy, it is rather difficult to comprehend why not one of today's psychics has borrowed his or her predictions from biblical prophecy. Can it be because their sources of inspiration are opposed to one another even though the predictions display certain similarities? Modern psychics claim to have the same gift of prophecy as the biblical prophets of old, and they use the Bible to substantiate their claims, but instead of drawing on the rich source of the Bible, they borrow from other psychics whose accuracies are spoken of only in degrees or percentages of degrees. Somehow they have missed the greatest prophetic handbook of all.

The prophets of old believed in continuous revelation. It is interesting to note that the same prophetic books in which were recorded the timely warnings of the patriarchal

The Far-Reaching Visions of John of Patmos

prophets also contain forecasts for a time in the future when, according to the prophet Joel, prophecy and prophets, both male and female, will again occupy a pivotal place in our lives: "And afterward, I will pour out my Spirit on all people. Your sons and daughters will prophesy, your old men will dream dreams, your young men will see visions."

Two great prophets of biblical times, Daniel and John, left us more information about the destiny of this world than all the others combined, and their end-of-time visions still rank as the most significant of all. Daniel's visions appear to have a deeper religious and political meaning, while those of John of Patmos are more concerned with prophecy as it applies to the destiny of individuals. His book, known as Revelation, is a compilation of mysteries that unfold slowly as reason is applied to its complex symbolism.

John received his visions while a prisoner on the Greek island of Patmos, a small, barren, rocky island about forty miles off the southwest coast of Asia Minor. Textual and historical evidence places his writings near the end of the reign of the Roman emperor Domitian (A.D. 81–96), a merciless tyrant whose chief aim in life seemed to be the persecution of the early Christians.

Exiled to Patmos by the Roman oppressors, John received a number of revelations. Because they dealt with an unveiling of the future, they have become known as apocalyptic writings. Today's psychics stand in awe of what was disclosed to him, for they sense that their own visions are far inferior to what was revealed to the old Christian seer in exile. They'd love to be able to compare their gifts of prophecy to his, but somehow they don't dare.

John was a deeply spiritual man, totally unlike Nostradamus who was a medical doctor who dabbled in astrology and the other occult sciences. John has often been identified as the former disciple of Jesus and author of the

Gospel according to John, which sets him apart from Nostradamus, Jeane Dixon, David Bubar, Criswell, Daniel Logan, and other seers.

Even the manner in which his visions were revealed to him differed from that of today's seers. His revelations were not accompanied by the flickering of lights in a chandelier (Dixon) or dependent upon the inspiration of a spirit medium (Daniel Logan); he was not immersed in the occult sciences (Nostradamus), nor did he gaze into the shimmering depths of a crystal ball (Irene Hughes). John's visions have the touch of authenticity, of being inspired by the true source of prophecy.

After explaining that he had been exiled to Patmos as part of the religious persecution, John relayed how, during meditation, he was startled by a loud voice behind him that instructed him to write down what would be revealed to him in vision. John whirled around, listened, and stood transfixed, later on entrusting what he saw to his scroll:

> I saw seven golden lampstands, and among the lampstands was someone 'like a son of man,' dressed in a robe reaching down to his feet and with a golden sash around his chest.
>
> His head and hair were like wool, as white as snow, and his eyes were like blazing fire. His feet were like bronze glowing in a furnace, and his voice was like the sound of rushing waters.
>
> In his right hand he held seven stars, and out of his mouth came a sharp double-edged sword. His face was like the sun shining in all its brilliance.
>
> When I saw him, I fell at his feet as though dead. Then he placed his right hand on me and said: "Do not be afraid. I am the First and the Last. I am the Living One; I was dead, and behold I am alive for

ever and ever! And I hold the keys of death and Hades."

Obviously this mysterious being is Jesus, whose crucifixion John had witnessed some sixty years earlier. John says that he resembled the "Son of Man" (Jesus' favorite name for himself), but he also recorded the words "I was dead, and behold I am alive for ever and ever! And I hold the keys of death and Hades." John therefore believed his source of inspiration to be the Son of God, a claim no modern psychic prophet has ever dared to make.

What followed from that moment on has become the subject of endless interpretations and has formed the basis for some of the major doctrines of many of the world's religions. This book will not deal with the theology of John's visions but rather with some of his visions involving the end of time.

Halfway into his vision, John noticed four mysterious creatures that could have come directly from Greek or Roman mythology:

> They were covered with eyes, in front and in back. The first living creature was like a lion, the second was like an ox, the third had a face like a man, the fourth was like a flying eagle.
> Each of the four living creatures had six wings and was covered with eyes all around, even under his wings.

THE SEVEN SEALS

Soon John saw another scene. The Son of Man, who had called him into the vision, had now taken on the appearance of a recently slain lamb and had been presented with a scroll with writing on both sides, sealed with seven seals. And while John watched, the lamb tore off the first seal and with a voice like thunder, one of the four living creatures shouted, "Come!" And at that moment a White Horse appeared before John, its rider bearing a crown and holding a bow in his hand, riding as if headed for conquest.

When the second seal was opened, another one of the four creatures cried, "Come!" and this time a fiery red horse appeared. Its rider was given a large sword together with the power to take peace from the earth and make men slay one another.

The opening of the third seal was accompanied by a shout of "Come" from the third mysterious creature, after which a black horse appeared on the scene. Its rider was holding a pair of scales. John commented, "Then I heard what sounded like a voice among the four living creatures, saying, 'A quart of wheat for a day's wages, and three quarts of barley for a day's wages, and do not damage the oil and the wine!'

"When the Lamb opened the fourth seal," John recalls, "I heard the voice of the fourth living creature say, 'Come!' I looked, and there before me was a pale horse! Its rider was named Death, and Hades was following close behind him. They were given power over a fourth of the earth to kill by sword, famine and plague, and by the wild beasts of the earth."

The opening of the fifth seal released a loud cry emanating from the souls of a multitude of those who had been tortured for religious reasons, demanding, "How long, Sovereign Lord, holy and true, until you judge the inhabitants of the earth and avenge our blood?"

When the sixth seal was opened, nature finally began to respond: "There was a great earthquake. The sun turned black like sackcloth made of goat hair, the whole moon turned blood red, and the stars in the sky fell to earth, as late figs drop from a fig tree when shaken by a strong wind. The sky receded like a scroll, rolling up, and every mountain and island was removed from its place."

But with the opening of the seventh and final seal, a long silence ensued, after which seven angels received seven trumpets. Then John noticed still another angel who took a censer, filled it with fire from the altar, and hurled it on the earth; creating "peals of thunder, rumblings, flashes of lightning and an earthquake."

Students of prophecy see in the vision of the Four Horsemen a progressive view of worsening world conditions, with the first three horses symbolizing the growth of the early Christian church, while the pale horse, the fourth and last one, signifies the final period of distress for the human race. John saw that it was given "power over a fourth part of the earth, to kill with sword, and with hunger, and with death, and with the beasts of the earth." This shows the bloody and brutal nature of the final days. Each horseman is thought to represent a historical period marked by specific historical, religious, political, or natural developments.

John's prophecy was undoubtedly inspired by the same source who forecast the end of the world in Matthew 24. Note especially the details supplied in verses 29 and 30, even though Matthew's predictions were written ninety-eight years after the birth of Christ:

> Immediately after the distress of those days the sun will be darkened, and the moon will not give its light; the stars will fall from the sky, and the heavenly bodies will be shaken.
>
> At that time the sign of the Son of Man will appear in the sky, and all the nations of the earth will mourn.

The sixth seal called for an earthquake, the sun turning black like sackcloth, the moon turning red, and the stars falling from the skies, followed by one last great all-destructive earthquake to be felt at the second coming of Christ. Interpreters of prophecy assume that, inasmuch as the four major signs of the sixth seal are grouped together in two short verses, they should follow one another in order and within a relatively short period of time. Four of the five major signs have found fulfillment in precisely that way.

Historically no other time span during the last few centuries fits as accurately as the seventy-eight years between November 1, 1755, and November 13, 1833.

The Great Earthquake

The most striking fulfillment of this first-century prophecy, the great earthquake, took place on November 1, 1755, when an earthquake hit Lisbon, Portugal, with tremendous force, destroying a vast area. Robert Sears writes:

> The great earthquake of 1755 extended over a tract of at least four millions of square miles. Its effects were even extended to the waters, in many places where the shocks were not perceptible. It pervaded the greater portion of the continents of Europe, Africa and America; but its extreme violence was exercised on the southwestern part of the former.
>
> In Africa, this earthquake was felt almost as severely as it had been in Europe. A great part of the city of Algiers was destroyed. Many houses were thrown down at Fez and Mequinez, and multitudes were buried beneath their ruins. . . . It is probable that all Africa was shaken by this tremen-

dous convulsion. At the north, it extended to Norway and Sweden; Germany, Holland, France, Great Britain, and Ireland were all more or less agitated by the same great and terrible commotion of the elements.... The city of Lisbon ... previous to that calamity ... contained about 150,000 inhabitants.... [About] 90,000 persons are supposed to have been lost on that fatal day.

The shock of the earthquake was instantly followed by the fall of every church and convent, almost all the large public buildings and more than one fourth of the houses. In about two hours after the shock, fires broke out in different quarters, and raged with such violence for the space of nearly three days that the city was completely desolated. ... The terror of the people was beyond description. Nobody wept; it was beyond tears. They ran hither and thither, delirious with horror and astonishment, beating their faces and breasts, crying "Misericordia! The world's at an end!" In the course of about six minutes sixty thousand persons perished. The sea first retired, and laid the bar dry. It then rolled in, rising fifty feet above its ordinary level. The mountains ... were impetuously shaken, as it were, from their very foundations; and some of them opened at their summits which were split and rent in a wonderful manner, huge masses of them being thrown down into the subadjacent valleys. Even in Britain the quake was felt with great intensity.

Other earthquakes have caused even greater devastation in localized areas, but never before or since has one earthquake covered so many millions of square miles.

A.D. 2000

And the Sun Became Black as Sackcloth

If the Lisbon earthquake was the beginning of the series of extraordinary events forecast by John, then the second one should be the blackened sun—and indeed it was. It happened twenty-five years after the Lisbon quake, and since that time it has been known as the "darkest day in history."

Noah Webster reported that "the obscuration began about ten o'clock in the morning, and continued till the middle of the next night, but with differences of degree and duration in different places. . . . The true cause of this remarkable phenomenon is not known."

Another witness described the happening as follows:

> In the morning the sun rose clear, but was soon overcast. The clouds became lowery, and from them black and ominous, as they soon appeared, lightning flashed, thunder rilled, and a little rain fell. Toward nine o'clock, the clouds became thinner, and assumed a brassy or coppery appearance, and earth, rocks, trees, buildings, water, and persons were changed by this strange, unearthly light. A few minutes later, a heavy black cloud spread over the entire sky except a narrow rim at the horizon, and it was as dark as it usually is at nine o'clock on a summer evening. . . .
>
> Fear, anxiety, and awe gradually filled the minds of the people. Women stood at the door, looking out upon the dark landscape; men returned from their labor in the fields; the carpenter left his tools, the blacksmith his forge, the tradesman his counter. Schools were dismissed, and tremblingly the children fled homeward. Travelers put up at the nearest farmhouse. "What is com-

ing?" queried every lip and heart. It seemed as if a hurricane was about to dash across the land, or as if it was the day of the consummation of all things.

Candles were used; and hearth fires shone as brightly as on a moonless evening in autumn. . . . Fowls retired to their roosts and went to sleep, cattle gathered at the pasture bars and lowed, frogs peeped, birds sang their evening songs, and bats flew about. But the human knew that night had not yet come.

More precise information came from Samuel William, a professor:

> *The time* of this extraordinary darkness was May 19, 1780. It came on between the hours of ten and eleven A.M., and continued until the middle of the next night, but with different appearances at different places.
> *The degree* to which the darkness arose was different at different places. In most parts of the country it was so great that people were unable to read common print, determine the time of day by their clocks or watches, dine, or manage their domestic business without the light of candles.
> *The extent* of this darkness was very remarkable. Our intelligence in this respect is not so particular as I could wish; but from the accounts that have been received, it seems to have extended all over the New England states. It was observed as far east as Falmouth [a town north of Portland, Maine]. To the westward we hear of its reaching to the farthest parts of Connecticut and Albany. To the southward it was observed all along the seacoasts, and to the north as far as our settlements extend.

It is probable it extended much beyond these limits in some directions, but the exact boundaries cannot be ascertained by any observations that I have been able to collect.

With regard to its duration it continued in this place at least fourteen hours; but it is probable this was not exactly the same in different parts of the country.

The appearance and effects were such as tended to make the prospect extremely dull and gloomy. Candles were lighted up in the houses, the birds, having sung their evening songs, disappeared, and became silent; the fowls retired to roost; the cocks were crowing all around, as at the break of day; objects could not be distinguished but at a very little distance; and everything bore the appearance and gloom of night.

Still, as the evening of that dreadful day was drawing to a close, only two of the events forecast in Revelation had occurred, and I seriously question whether casual students of prophecy would consider any possible connection between these and the prophecy of the sixth seal. However, to the more than casual observer, the night of May 19, 1780, brought the third phenomenon—in conformity with John's prophetic vision—which was just as unusual as the day that had just ended.

The Moon Turned to Blood

The intense darkness of the day was succeeded, an hour or two before evening, by a partially clear sky. Then the sun appeared, although obscured by a heavy black mist. This changed after sundown as the ominous clouds returned and once again covered the land with darkness. By now the dark had become frightful and oppressive, and even though there was almost a full moon, no object was discernible without the aid of artificial light, which, when seen from the neighboring houses and other places at a distance, appeared almost impervious to the rays.

"The darkness . . . was probably as gross as ever has been observed since the Almighty first gave birth to light," the official records state. "I could not help conceiving at the time, that if a very luminous body in the universe had been shrouded in impenetrable shades, or struck out of existence, the darkness could not have been more complete. A sheet of white paper held within a few inches of the eyes, was equally invisible with the blackest velvet."

The darkness held until approximately one o'clock, and even though the moon occasionally became visible after nine, it did nothing to dissipate the blackness that had covered the sky, for whenever it was seen, it had the appearance of blood. This darkness was not caused by an eclipse, according to the records for that year and in view of the fact that the moon been full on the previous night. In fact, no natural phenomenon could have accounted for the quick succession of events.

A Rain of Stars

The prophet John had not specified that all four signs would occur within a few years, yet three of them reached complete and accurate fulfillment within only twenty-five years. Students of prophecy anxiously awaited the fulfillment of the fourth. A generation passed before it happened, but when it did, it created an awesome spectacle.

Never before had prophetic power displayed its authority as impressively as when the stars fell from heaven on

November 13, 1833. A reporter for the *New York Journal of Commerce* later wrote an eyewitness account of the fulfillment of the fourth sign:

> At the cry, "Look out of the window," I sprang from a deep sleep, and with wonder saw the east lighted up with the dawn and meteors. . . . I called my wife to behold; and while robing, she exclaimed, "See how the stars fall!" I replied, "That is the wonder," and we felt in our hearts that it was a sign of the last days. For truly "the stars of heaven fell unto the earth, even as a fig tree casteth her untimely figs, when she is shaken of a mighty wind."
>
> And how did they fall? Neither myself nor one of the family heard any report; and were I to hunt through nature for a simile, I could not find one so apt to illustrate the appearance of the heavens, as that which St. John uses in the prophecy before quoted. . . . The falling of the stars did not come, as if from several trees shaken, but from one; those which appeared in the east fell toward the east; those which appeared in the north fell toward the north; those which appeared in the west fell toward the west; and those which appeared in the south (for I went out of my residence into the park), fell toward the south; and they fell, not as ripe fruit falls. Far from it. But they flew, they were cast, like the unripe fruit, which at first refuses to leave the branch; and, when it does break its hold, flies swiftly, straight off, descending; and in the multitude falling, some cross the track of others, as they are thrown with more or less force.
>
> It seemed as if the whole starry heavens had congregated at one point near the zenith, and were

simultaneously shooting forth, with the velocity of lightning, to every part of the horizon; and yet they were not exhausted—thousands swiftly followed in the tracks of thousands, as if they had been created for the occasion.

No celestial phenomenon has ever occurred in this country, since its first settlement, which was viewed with such intense admiration by one class in the community, or with such dread and alarm by another. Its sublimity and awful beauty still linger in many minds. . . . Never did rain fall much thicker than the meteors fell toward the earth; east, west, north, and south, it was the same. In a word, the whole heavens seemed in motion. . . . From two o'clock until broad daylight, the sky being perfectly serene and cloudless, an incessant play of dazzling brilliant luminosities was kept up in the whole heavens.

The whole heavens seemed in motion, and suggested to some the awful grandeur of the image employed in the Apocalypse, upon the opening of the Sixth Seal, when "the stars of heaven fell unto the earth."

The wonder caused Denison Olmsted to comment as follows:

The shower pervaded nearly the whole of North America, having appeared in nearly equal splendor from the British possessions on the north, to the West Indian Islands and Mexico on the south, and from sixty-one degrees of longitude east of the American coast, quite to the Pacific Ocean on the west. Throughout this immense region, the duration was nearly the same. The meteors began to attract attention by their unusual frequency and brilliance, from nine to twelve o'clock in the evening; were most striking in their appearance from two to five; arrived at their maximum, in many places, about four o'clock; and continued until rendered invisible by the light of day.

The reader may imagine a constant succession of fire balls, resembling sky rockets, radiating in all directions from a point in the heavens, a few degrees south of the zenith, and following the arch of the sky towards the horizon. . . . The balls, as they traveled down the vault, usually left after them a vivid streak of light, and just before they disappeared, exploded, or suddenly resolved themselves, into smoke. No report or noise of any kind was observed, although we listened intently.

The spectator was presented with meteors of various sizes and degrees of splendor; some were mere points, but others were larger and brighter than Jupiter or Venus; and one, seen by a credible witness before the writer was called, was judged to be nearly as large as the moon. The flashes of light, although less intense than lightning, were so bright as to awaken people in their beds. One ball that shot off in the northwest direction, and exploded a little northward of the star Capella, left, just behind the place of explosion, a phosphorescent train of peculiar beauty.

Seldom has prophecy been fulfilled so clearly and with such great accuracy. It changed the lives of many of those who witnessed the cosmic spectacle, for they felt the coming of the Man of Peace would soon be at hand.

The Seven Trumpets

John's attention was directed toward the seven angels who were holding the seven trumpets they had received when the seventh seal was broken. Amid peals of thunder and lightning the first angel ominously raised his instrument and blew:

> The first angel sounded his trumpet and there came hail and fire mixed with blood, and it was hurled down upon the earth. A third of the earth was burned up, a third of the trees were burned up, and all the green grass was burned up.
>
> The second angel sounded his trumpet, and something like a huge mountain, all ablaze, was thrown into the sea. A third of the sea turned into blood, a third of the living creatures in the sea died, and a third of the ships were destroyed.
>
> The third angel sounded his trumpet, and a great star, blazing like a torch, fell from the sky on a third of the rivers and on the springs of water—the name of the star is Wormwood. A third of the waters turned bitter, and many people died from the waters that had become bitter.
>
> The fourth angel sounded his trumpet, and a third of the sun was struck, a third of the moon, and a third of the stars, so that a third of them turned dark. A third of the day was without light, and also a third of the night.

Awed by so much devastation, John watched in silence as the vision continued to unfold and the voice of an eagle cried, "Woe! Woe! Woe to the inhabitants of the earth, because of the trumpet blasts about to be sounded by the other three angels!"

The calamities that John predicted and those that were made by Nostradamus are too similar to be ignored. There is little doubt that the deaths (blood) caused by the hail (unnatural winterlike conditions), followed by a severe and prolonged drought (firelike conditions), will be the direct cause for a burning up of one-third of all the trees left on this planet as well as one-third of all the grazing lands. Dense clouds of smoke, air pollution, starvation, and unbearable global weather conditions will create havoc for everyone who manages to escape the first onslaught.

Our world is threatened by the presence of the five hundred live volcanos situated along the Ring of Fire, and it does not take much imagination to see in the "huge mountain, all ablaze" that was "thrown into the sea" a major volcanic eruption that will kill indiscriminately. John's words indicate that most of its effects will be felt at sea; hence we should expect a major volcanic eruption on an island or close to the coast of one of the major seas.

John's description of the third angel seems to be the precursor of the Nostradamian prediction of the giant comet that is to hit the Indian Ocean. Nostradamus predicted that the coming of the meteor will result in famine caused by the tremendous "heat," which will be so severe that "fish will be boiled in the lakes." What better description for a "falling star" than a "great star from heaven that has the appearance of a lamp." The heat and ash of the sizzling comet will destroy fish and other ocean creatures in their natural habitat, people will die by the hundreds of thousands because of the water pollution, and thousands of ships will be unable to escape the holocaust and resulting tidal waves. With the sounding of the third trumpet, as witnessed by John, the sun, moon, and stars will lose one-third of their light causing darkness to cover the globe.

The Far-Reaching Visions of John of Patmos

No one knows the time element involved in the fulfillment of the four trumpets prophecy, but it is reasonable to assume that all four of them will fall within one generation. In fact some interpreters even are convinced that they will follow one another in rapid sequence, perhaps in as short a time span as one year.

The devastation, drought, pollution, and famine that will start with the first trumpet will be augmented by the unequaled volcanic eruption that will practically boil parts of the ocean, pollute the waters, and destroy a great part of the merchant fleets of the industrial nations, thereby greatly aggravating the hunger problem.

Amid the political and economic turmoil this will create, the news that a "great star" is falling from heaven and is heading for the Indian Ocean will create near panic among the already desperate earth population. Swinging its fiery tail, the comet will head for our globe, creating earthquakes and gigantic tidal waves upon its impact. Mile-high clouds of steam, smoke, and dust will rise into the atmosphere. These clouds will encircle the earth. The sun will be obscured behind a black barrier, and its heating rays will be unable to reach the earth's surface, eventually causing a drop in the world's temperatures, making life even more miserable.

After a while the dust particles will return to earth with the incessant rains caused by the changing weather. This will poison streams and drinking water supplies as the polluted rain mixes with the rivers and streams.

The lack of adequate food and clean water and the unusually unpredictable climate will cause countless people to die of starvation, pollution, or exposure to extreme heat or cold. In other words, the world will have become unfit for human habitation.

Yet John saw this as only the beginning, with more, much more, to follow.

The next two trumpet blasts followed in quick succession. At the sound of the first of the two, another star fell from heaven, causing smoke to rise up as from a gigantic furnace. And out of the smoke came locusts looking like horses prepared for battle, with faces resembling human heads with lion's teeth, and assigned to torture that part of humanity whose wickedness could no longer be ignored.

Often, when reading prophetic symbolism, we try to find an interpretation that fits a preconceived idea. But do we necessarily have to take the locusts as a *symbolic* threat? An article in the *New York Times* in 1976 focused attention on the threat posed by locusts in the Middle East and Africa. The article mentioned three different occasions in the last hundred years on which swarming locusts threatened all life for hundreds of miles. The article relates how a "swarm of locusts some 2,600 square miles in area, crossed the Red Sea in what amounted to a re-enactment of one of the biblical plagues of Egypt." Locusts also posed a severe threat during World War II when sudden swarms seriously interfered with important military operations in the Middle East. The article concluded that peculiar environmental conditions are often the cause of these sudden plagues. Maybe the locusts in Revelation are not a symbol at all. Perhaps the prophecy just meant what it said!

When the sixth trumpet finally sounded, John saw a mounted army of 200 million supernatural beings released to do battle against the inhabitants of the earth, and "to kill a third of mankind."

John did not recognize the weapons used, but did see that the third of mankind that was being killed died from the sulfur, smoke, and fire released from the mouths and the tails of the horses (self-propelled vehicles of war?). John must have been horrified at the carnage which followed, for killing one-third of humanity meant annihilating approximately 1.3 billion people in a relatively short period of time, all as part of God's retribution against humanity.

That much of what John saw was beyond his comprehension is understandable. He could only relate the images and symbols he saw in his vision to what he knew to exist in real life, and his world was far removed from our twentieth-century technology. Still in a trance, John watched world history being arranged in advance, serving as a chosen witness.

Finally the seventh angel sounded his trumpet, and John saw seven other angels holding seven bowls filled with the wrath of God, each one representing a plague that would be poured out over mankind as a last warning. Many eschatologists believe the seven plagues that are to scourge the human race on the threshold of the end of time will follow one another quickly, running their course within nine months to a year, affecting a frightened people who have already been hit hard by a generation of supernaturally caused calamities.

Filled with the growing conviction that he was slowly being initiated into the judgments of God, John listened in fascination as a loud voice commanded the angels to pour out the seven bowls of wrath upon the earth:

> The first angel went and poured out his bowl on the land, and ugly and painful sores broke out on the people who had the mark of the beast and worshiped his image.
>
> The second angel poured out his bowl on the seas, and it turned into blood like that of a dead man, and every living thing in the sea died.
>
> The third angel poured out his bowl on the rivers and springs of water, and they became blood.

The fourth angel poured out his bowl on the sun, and the sun was given power to scorch people.

The fifth angel poured out his bowl on the throne of the beast, and his kingdom was plunged into darkness. Men gnawed their tongues in agony and cursed the God of heaven because of their pains and their sores, but they refused to repent of what they had done.

The sixth angel poured out his bowl on the great river Euphrates, and its water was dried up to prepare the way for the kings from the East. . . . Then they gathered the kings together to the place that in Hebrew is called Armageddon.

We will never know the extent of the horror and pity that engulfed the seer's mind as he watched the vision of a generation that had already suffered so much being exposed to a torture that was excruciating, both physically and mentally.

Already cringing in fear and pain from the horrors of war, famine, drought, and disease, they now became infected with the curse of the first plague—painful and ugly sores. With the rivers and wells already heavily polluted, the only water sources they could turn to were the oceans and seas. Yet the second plague changed all that by turning the seas into blood. A return to the polluted rivers and stream was also out of the question for the third plague had already changed them, too.

Diseased, feverish, waterless, starved, and filthy, human beings were finding their existence worthless. And to compound the curse and its effect, the fourth angel poured the fourth plague over the suffering world, giving the sun power to scorch and burn: "The fifth angel poured out his bowl on the throne of the beast, and his kingdom was plunged into darkness. Men gnawed their tongues in agony and cursed the God of heaven because of their pains and their sores, but they refused to repent of what they had done."

Will anyone ever be able to describe the horror, tumult, desperation, fear, and indescribable torment that will be experienced by all those who will be the recipient of the plagues of the wrath of the Creator?

Yet the long-expected Battle of Armageddon, the war to end all wars, as part of the sixth plague of John's prophecy, also foreseen by Nostradamus, will have to be fought by that debilitated and diseased generation.

Can anything be more horrible?

6
Humanity's Rush to Judgment

> Man is like the foam of the sea, that floats upon the surface of the water. When the wind blows, it vanishes, as if it had never been. Thus are our lives blown away by Death.
>
> —Kahlil Gibran

Human beings have never been patient, and the uncertainty of the future has not added to their feelings of security.

Over the years we have seen prophecies unfold and have watched the strides of technological advancement shrink our world. We are no longer able to ignore the dangers that are approaching; we're rapidly running out of sand in which to bury our heads. It would seem that subconsciously we've decided to end it all. For many of us, leaving it up to supernatural intervention or a natural catastrophe just isn't good enough anymore. We still want to be the masters of our own destiny, and, having made this choice, we have positioned ourselves squarely on the threshold of extinction, ready to destroy what our ancestors so carefully preserved for us.

The sense of approaching doom can be felt everywhere, and the nuclear arms race has greatly affected humanity's subconscious quest for a way out. In 1980, Exit, a London-based organization, published *A Guide to Self-Deliverance*, a 10,000-word manual that explains clearly and matter-of-factly how to commit suicide! The United States quickly came out with its own version, *Let Me Die before I Wake*. Brisk sales were reported for both publications, but aside from being another signal to the deeply depressed that they now have a foolproof way out of their dilemma, the books provided no solution to the real problems that confront us.

People are finding ways to cope with the growing threat of annihilation—whatever the cause may be. The fear of nuclear war has been with us since 1945, yet our anxiety over it acquired a kind of nostalgic quaintness with the passing of the 1950s. The ban-the-bomb rallies, the fallout shelters, the evacuation signs, and even the classroom drills now seem childishly inadequate. Suddenly, however, these fears have taken on a new perspective. The deployment of American Pershing II missiles in Western Europe has taken the romance out of warfare and put its horror onto the mastheads of the morning papers.

We're beginning to run scared. Fear is beginning to affect the younger generation, too. Their innocent expectations of happiness are mixed with the fear of nuclear death. *Newsweek* reports that an Iowa City eighth grader, Leigh Ann Kennedy, recently polled 370 of her contemporaries and found that 75 percent of them think about nuclear war often, 66 percent are scared because of it, and 57 percent feel helpless to do anything about it. "We're up the creek without a paddle, and I'll be blown away before I am thirty years old," wrote one anonymous respondent. Theology teacher West Cosgrove of Houston's St. Thomas High School reports that 95 percent of the freshmen attending a history of war presentation said they doubted they'd live to be forty years old.

Already the warnings contained in the *Global 2000 Report*, published in 1980 as the result of a study commissioned by President Carter, are being viewed as bleak and insignificant. The problems predicted in *Global 2000* may never materialize because of our rush to judgment.

Blatantly ignoring the lessons contained in the *Mahabharata*, we recklessly toyed with the atom, and in doing so unleashed a holocaust the results of which are now beginning to worry us. Instead of muzzling the hounds of war, we have cut them loose.

The result is that we are now on the verge of destroying our own civilization in a manner that is consistent with our lack of self-control. Our fear that our beautiful planet may be destroyed by a series of natural catastrophes has a sound basis in both predictions and scientific facts. But the man-made threat of annihilation by nuclear fire is even more realistic and probably even closer at hand. By latest count ten nations have the capability to build nuclear devices, and as the number of countries with nuclear weapons increases, so does the likelihood of a nuclear war.

The latest figures for the United States alone show that the government's spending for nuclear warheads grew from $3 billion in 1980 to about $5.7 billion in 1983. This, however, is expected to rise to $6.8 billion in 1984. Will this increase our feeling of security in this insecure world? What will it do but increase the overkill?

A.D. 2000

The fear of being charred by a nuclear fire ball is almost totally erasing the fear of being extinguished by the supernatural catastrophies predicted by John and Nostradamus.

World War II is now history and statistics, and one of the figures that has come forth from that cruel contest is that the total explosive power of all the bombs used in that conflict is the equivalent of 2 million tons of TNT, *the same explosive power as can now be found in one simple strategic nuclear warhead.* Who can feel safe in a world where more than 50,000 nuclear warheads of different sizes representing more than 13,000 megatons (million tons) of TNT, enough to obliterate a million Hiroshimas, are waiting to be unleashed? But there are not a million cities the size of Hiroshima; in fact, there are only about three thousand cities with a population over 100,000, and if only one of these bombs were thrown on each of these cities, there would still be 47,000 warheads left to be used on other "deserving" targets. And who will guarantee that the nuclear arsenal will not grow even larger? Developing and producing nuclear warheads is one of the most rapidly expanding businesses in this country. "The government is building a whole new generation of nuclear weapons simultaneously," says Bill Hartung, an analyst for the Council on Economic Priorities, "and it wants new warheads for all of them!"

So where are we headed? Can we wait for the prophetically promised naturally or supernaturally inspired calamities, or are we going to ignite our own holocaust and brutally rip open the globe and create our own doomsday? Our very own A.D. 2000 far ahead of schedule?

To ensure the survival of the United States in case of an all-out nuclear confrontation with the USSR, American war-planners convene once a year to "play" their doomsday exercise, a nuclear war strategy where even the winner becomes a loser. During one of the most recent computerized wars, war gamers staged an extensive simulation of a superpower showdown. For five days the doomsday scenario was played around a 5,000-megaton missile attack supposedly launched against the U.S. mainland. When it was all over the United States had managed to set in motion an all-out retaliatory strike even after absorbing the Soviet onslaught.

The planners considered this a military victory of sorts, but even though it assured them that the government could keep functioning under an all-out Soviet assault, it did not answer the question as to whether the planet would survive.

A study released in 1983 by the World Health Organization scrutinized the effects of a nuclear war on the world population. Chaired by Sune K. Bergstrom, the study indicated that such a war would kill at least 1.1 billion people in the USSR, the United States, China, Europe, and Japan within a matter of minutes. For the billion or more who were injured, there would be no adequate medical help, resulting in a number of indirect casualties equaling those caused by direct hit.

If this war should happen within the next few years, about half of the world population would be destroyed by nuclear fire. The survivors would have to live on a globe seared by heat and exposed to a slow death by radiation or starvation. The human race might survive such a torturous holocaust, but this isn't all there is to it. A recent study indicates that the long-term environmental impact of a major nuclear war would make life on earth almost impossible because of the changes it would cause in the world's climate.

The study had its origin in observations made by the U.S. Mariner spacecraft, which arrived in the vicinity of the planet Mars during the latter part of 1971. From there it transmitted information back to earth indicating that the "red planet" had become the center of a dust storm. The particles of dust were still slowly descending to the surface of the planet.

Because of its density, the thick layer of dust had partially blocked the incoming sunlight, thereby cooling the surface of the planet. Eventually, after the storm died down and the dust resettled on Mars, the planet's temperature gradually returned to normal. The spacecraft-to-earth transmissions, however, carried with them telltale information about the temperature changes and thus presented our scientists with sufficient data on which to base conclusions about the atmospheric consequences of a nuclear war.

The result, a scientific paper entitled "Global Atmospheric Consequences of Nuclear War," was written by a team of Earth scientists: Carl Sagan, director of planetary studies at Cornell University; Owen B. Toon, Thomas P. Ackerman, and James B. Pollack of the National Aeronautics and Space Administration; and Richard P. Turco of R&D Associates. It is known as the TAPPS report, from the first letters of the authors' last names. Often the findings of scientists are presented in dry and hard-to-read volumes filled with scientific jargon, but both the language and the implications of this report are frighteningly clear.

Many computer studies of the effects of nuclear attacks have been based on yields of 1,000 to 5,000 megatons. The computer model used by the TAPPS team had a base line of 5,000 megatons, which would allow the United States and the USSR to hit each other with an overkill of 2,500 megatons. Furthermore, for the sake of the study it was assumed that only 20 percent of the total firepower would be used on industrial targets or population centers.

Using the experiences of the planet Mars as guideline, the ultimate results of the study far exceeded the worst expectations. The study revealed, for example, that because of the dust and smoke generated by the nuclear blasts and the length of time it would remain in the atmosphere, blocking the heating rays of the sun from reaching the surface of the earth, the amount of sunlight that would come through would be reduced to only a few percent of its normal intensity. For weeks on end a dismal gloom would cover the Northern Hemisphere. The constant darkness would be so intense and of such long duration that plant life would die and the stench of rotten vegetation would mix with the foul odor of more than one billion burned and putrifying bodies.

But this is not the end of the scenario by far. The report also indicates that because of the interfering cloud layer, the earth's temperatures would soon drop to a low of $-25°C$. and remain far below the freezing point for several months, even if the war were fought during the hot months of summer. All livestock would freeze and die; crops would wither in the fields, and those who had survived the blasts would starve.

Says Dr. Sagan, a principal researcher on the project:

> The cold, the dark and the intense radioactivity, together lasting for months, represent a severe assault on our civilization and our species. Civil and sanitary services would be wiped out. Medical facilities, drugs, the most rudimentary means for relieving the vast human suffering, would be unavailable. Any but the most elaborate shelters would be useless, quite apart from the question of what good it might be to emerge a few months later. Synthetics burned in the destruction of the cities would produce a wide variety of toxic gases including carbon monoxide, cyanides, dioxins and furans. After the dust and soot settled out, the solar ultraviolet flux would be much larger than its present value. Immunity to disease would decline. Epidemics and pandemics would be rampant, es-

pecially after the billion or so unburied bodies began to thaw.

Even if a nuclear war should be fought with only 100 megatons of nuclear explosive power, we would still face approximately the same situation. The thousands of burning cities and forests would produce sufficient smoke, dust, and soot to create a thick cloud layer, resulting in the same dire effects, killing us off as surely as the predictions of Nostradamus and John's prophecies promised.

Sagan comments rather sadly,

> Our results have been carefully scrutinized by more than 100 scientists in the United States, Europe and the Soviet Union. There are still arguments on points of detail. But the overall conclusion seems to be agreed upon: There are severe and previously unanticipated global consequences of nuclear war—subfreezing temperatures in a twilit radioactive gloom lasting for months or longer.

So what will it be and how will it end? What really *are* our chances of being destroyed by a combination of natural and supernatural disasters? Will we escape the fulfillment of the psychic predictions and survive, only to be judged at another time? And how do we relate all this to the Apocalypse of John of Patmos?

In discussing the events predicted to take place around the year A.D. 2000, we have studied the forecasts that have been handed down to us over a period of hundreds of years. Our choices are clearly defined but also clearly limited.

In tabulating and comparing the psychic predictions for the end of this century, we indeed find an astonishing similarity of both detail and expectation.

Source	Approximate Time	Details of Event
Buddhists	A.D. 2000	Religious awakening followed by the coming of Kalki, the god of peace
Christians	end of time A.D. 2000 (?)	Wars, plagues, social and political upheaval, followed by the end of the world and the second coming of Christ
Jeane Dixon	A.D. 2000	Calamities, religious awakening, coming of the Child of the East
Heraclitus the Greek	end of time	End of the World; end of all things
Hindus	A.D. 2000	Religious awakening, followed by the coming of Kalki, the god of peace
Hopi Indians	A.D. 2000	Warfare against Indians, help from the nations of ancient knowledge, and coming of the Man of Peace from the East
Iroquois Indians	A.D. 2000	Battle between good and bad serpents, coming of the Man of Hope

Source	Approximate Time	Details of Event
Jews	end of time	Wars, religious upheavals followed by the coming of the Messiah
Daniel Logan	A.D. 2000	Wars and coming of Child of the East
Saint Malachy	A.D. 2000	Crowning of Pope Peter of Rome after which the Awful Judge will come
Montezuma	A.D. 2000	Slaughter of Aztec nation, end of influence of Catholic church, coming of Man of Peace from the East
Muslims	A.D. 2000	Religious awakening followed by the coming of Mahdi, the Enlightened One
Nostradamus	A.D. 2000	World in upheaval, natural catastrophies, coming of King of Terror
Oglala Sioux	A.D. 2000	Trouble, then coming of savior of the nation from the East
Mother Shipton	A.D. 2000	Technological developments and wars

Source	Approximate Time	Details of Event
Tibetans	End of 13th Dalai Lama A.D. 2000 (?)	Arghati, king of the world, wars, and natural catastrophies
George Washington	Late 1900s	Last great war involving the United States
Zoastrian Vestas	A.D. 2000	Spiritual awakening followed by the coming of Saoshyant, the Man of Peace

There is no way to test the prophetic accuracy of the psychics of old, but trusting that the source of their inspiration is still the same, we can get an indication of the relative reliability of their predictions by matching them against the findings of modern research.

While doing research for my book *The Soul Hustlers*, I interviewed fifty leading American psychic practitioners to ascertain their beliefs, convictions, dependence on one another, and their prophetic accuracy. Those interviewed included psychic seers, faith healers, astrologers, mediums, clairvoyants, psychometrists, witches, and outright devil worshipers. Many of them claimed to be inspired by the same power that inspired the biblical prophets, yet only 26.4 percent of them believed that the biblical prophecies dealing with the end of the world were still valid. Also, only 25.5 percent of them adhered to the age-old belief that the second coming of Christ or the coming of a Man of Peace would coincide with the end of the world. When asked whether they had seen this or a similar event in a vision, 38.8 percent said yes. When asked if they agreed with the other psychics who had predicted that the end of the world would come at the end of this century, 61.6 percent said they did.

This brings us back to our basic question: How accurate are the predictions of today's psychics?

Those who have studied the predictions of the master psychic Nostradamus have reached the conclusion that he has an accuracy rate of between 86 and 91 percent—an unbelievably high degree of accuracy for someone whose source of inspiration appears to have been ungodly.

This subject arose in a discussion I had a number of years ago with Regis Riesenman, a well-known parapsychologist in Arlington, Virginia, and Dr. Riesenman made some frank statements. "I have studied psychics and prophets for more than fifty years," he stated matter-of-factly, "and have found fewer than twenty with an accuracy of eighty to eighty-five percent. No psychic I know has ever gone beyond that point!"

Other researchers support this conclusion, which indicates that in their predictive work, today's psychic prophets have enough failures to make total fulfillment of their claims highly questionable. It has to some extent become customary to judge prophets by their performance. Foretelling future events—delving into the uncharted corridors of time—falls within the realm of "forbidden" knowledge, except when the God-power directs and controls the phenomenon. This delving is mysterious, and, because of this, prophets have often been regarded as special confidants of the Almighty. Throughout the ages, many prophetic warnings have been recorded and many more psychic predictions have been made, but the failure of a number of their predictions to attain complete or even partial fulfillment has forced the psychics to retreat behind a purposely created veil of mystery, using their fulfilled predictions to shield them from unwarranted attention.

Let's face it. No one boasts about his or her failures in life, psychic prophets least of all, since they invariably claim to receive their information from a being with supreme intelligence. Nevertheless they are highly vulnerable because of their lack of accuracy.

Daniel Logan, a psychic from New York City, once angrily complained, "The attitude of the public is not that I am right eighty percent of the time, but that I am wrong twenty percent of the time. It seems that if the psychic gives clear evidence of a reasonable percentage of accuracy, then he has done something quite extraordinary. Given the circumstances in which the psychic works and the material with which he deals, it seems to be remarkable that I am able to maintain an accuracy of eighty percent."

No matter how he defends his gift, however, his inspiration does fail him at least 20 percent of the time. Jeane Dixon, the woman who launched America on its mid-twentieth-century fascination with psychic prophecy, also has had her failures. Although she is reputed to have reached accuracies of up to 85 percent, those who are cognizant of her tremendous number of unfulfilled predictions do not credit her with perhaps more than 25 percent accuracy today.

Peter Hurkos, the Dutch-American psychic who has often worked as an investigator for law enforcement agencies, has reached as high as 80 percent accuracy. Ingel Swan, Harold Sherman, M. D. Dijkshoorn, Olaf Johnsson, Penny South, Robert Strong, Robert Nelson, Edward Snedeker, and many others in the psychic prediction field also have varying rates of prophetic fulfillment. Although their excuses for their shortcomings may vary, all without exception lack total accuracy.

The legacy of psychic prophecy that has been handed us

is indeed built on a source of inspiration that is often highly debatable, and at best—as with Nostradamus—between 80 and 90 percent correct.

Biblical prophecy has a different reputation. Many leading eschatologists who have studied biblical prophecy have concluded that approximately 95 percent of it has already found total and unquestionable fulfillment.

The remaining 5 percent, which deals mainly with end-of-time predictions, appears to be in the process of being fulfilled. Eschatologists usually single out Daniel and John of Patmos as the prophets whose end-of-time forecasts are so closely matched to current political, religious, or economic developments that the odds are overwhelmingly in favor of the Bible prophets reaching a full 100 percent fulfillment.

But does prophecy actually *have* to be fulfilled? Do events take place because they have been prophesied? Or have they been predicted because it was known in advance that these developments would take place? I am sure the question has plagued humanity ever since the first prophetic utterance came true.

It may seem strange, but contrary to our method of judging the accuracy of the psychic prophets, no one has ever evaluated a biblical prophet on the basis of his hits or misses, even though each of them has unfulfilled prophecies. Does this perhaps mean that psychic prophets and biblical prophets are judged according to a double standard? Certainly not, but there is a distinct difference between a "conditional prophecy" as given in the biblical prophetic books and a "chance prediction" originating from a psychic source.

In the Bible there is an element of controlled uncertainty, known as "conditional prophecy," that has to be considered in every prophecy that deals with the response of people. The prophet Jeremiah (590 B.C.) allowed for this when he quoted his source of inspiration: "At any moment I may threaten to uproot a nation or a kingdom, to pull it down and destroy it. But if the nation which I have threatened turns back from its wicked ways, then I shall think better of the evil I had in mind to bring on it" (Jer. 18:7,9).

This clearly indicates that the only way to escape the wrath forecast in a biblical prophecy is to turn away from evil. Prophecies have never been made to threaten humanity's existence; they were and still are a means of indicating to human beings the will of a higher being. An intensive study of prophecy definitely shows that when the human element is drawn into the prophecy—when it concerns the behavior of people—the promise of reward or punishment is invariably conditional. You can almost say that when in ancient times a prophecy declaring doom, death, or destruction was pronounced over humankind, a full 180-degree turn to a change in behavior was the only possible means of escaping the threatened disaster. Each time this move was made, the prophecy was annulled. It did not fail; it became void. It was retracted by the Author of Prophecy.

But while this element of conditional prophecy may have applied to issues affecting the course of ancient nations, it can have no bearing whatsoever on the end-of-time prophecies as related to the destiny of the world in general. The major prophecies clearly indicate that a definite time limit has been set and that this is neither conditional nor retractable. These prophecies are deterministic in nature. John realized this when during his vision he was told: "These sayings are faithful and true; and the Lord God of the holy prophets sent his angel to show unto his servants the things which must shortly be done" (Rev. 22:6).

Even General Douglas MacArthur felt this when, during his address at the ceremony of the surrender of Japan, he remarked, "A new era is upon us . . . we have had our last chance. If we do not now devise some greater and more equitable system, Armageddon will be at our door."

And almost prophetically, Leland Stowe commented in his 1946 book, *While Time Remains,* "Those foremost world authorities who split the atom and made the bomb have assured us that Armageddon and Doomsday are now suspended over the heads of our generation."

What is there in John's prophecy about Armageddon that evokes so much fear, even in the minds of our military leaders? Is it indeed possible that Armageddon is practically upon us and that our mismanagement of the nuclear age will be the catalyst to doom and supply our share in the fulfillment of this ancient prophecy?

7
Armageddon: The End of Time?

> I'll be astounded if this planet is still going fifty years from now. I don't think we will reach 2000. It would be miraculous!
>
> —Alistair Cooke

There is something intriguing about the way statesmen and military leaders are beginning to examine the biblical prophecies of Armageddon. The utter brutality and cruelty of warfare are so far removed from the gentle words of the Sermon on the Mount or the Golden Rule that their interest would be totally out of place were it not for the battle plans for Armageddon contained in the prophecies of Daniel and John of Patmos.

Humanity has learned a lesson, but the wrong one.

World War I was fought in Europe while the rest of the world stood by.

World War II was fought in Europe, Asia, and Africa, and much of the world became involved for the first time.

Now the nuclear arms race is on, and everyone may have to fight everyone else—and no one sees a way to stop it.

The dilemma was summed up quite eloquently by the former president of France, Valéry Giscard d'Estaing when he lamented, "The world is unhappy. It is unhappy because it doesn't know where it is going and because it senses that, if it knew, it would discover that it was heading for disaster."

And this nagging fear of pending disaster has everyone concerned, even the military establishment, for the chances that the holocaust will be ignited before the target date are getting greater with each passing day. How close we are to the commencment of doomsday was revealed in April 1976 when word leaked out that the Israelis had hastily assembled thirteen atomic bombs during the crucial days of the Yom Kippur War of 1973 and had placed them in the hands of air force units that stood ready for the command to deliver.

According to Albert Einstein, time moves faster the farther we venture into space. Sadly enough, we don't have to leave our planet to experience that, for by learning to split the atom we have condensed our future so much that there may not even be a tomorrow in which to travel that far.

Andrei Sakharov, the Russian physicist, once warned that "the pulling of a few levers, the pushing of a few buttons, and the throwing of a few switches would result in the complete annihilation of every living thing on the earth." He ought to know, because the armament industries of his country and ours produce at least six hydrogen warheads every day—and no one really knows why, for by wrapping just one hydrogen bomb in cobalt and exploding it at just the right spot, we can annihilate almost everyone on earth.

It is this barbarous inventiveness that will undoubtedly catapult us into the Battle of Armageddon.

Just as the detonation of the first atomic bomb proved that the stories contained in the *Mahabharata* were not fictitious but based on fact, so has a comparison of certain prophetic passages made eschatologists aware that the Bible actually appears to contain blunt references of the use of nuclear power in the last days.

Our word *uranium* is derived from the Greek word *ouranoi*. Matthew used this same word when he stated that "the powers of the heavens [*ouranoi*] shall be shaken" (24:29). Also in 2 Peter 3:7, we find "the present heavens [*ouranoi*] and earth are reserved for fire." The case becomes even stronger in verse 10 when, referring to the end of the world, Peter states that "the heavens shall pass away with a great noise, and the elements shall melt with fervent heat, the earth also and the works that are therein shall be burned up."

Is it possible that this actually refers to the destructive powers of uranium, the only fire that can melt both the atmosphere and the earth at the same time? Even the old prophet Zechariah makes one think he must have witnessed something resembling nuclear war, for he wrote, "Behold the day of the Lord cometh. . . . The Lord will smite all the people that have fought against Jerusalem; their flesh shall consume away while they stand upon their feet, and their eyes shall consume away in their holes" (Zech.

14:1,12). The descriptions of the effects of the bombing of Hiroshima and Nagasaki in 1945 contain passages too similar to Zechariah's prophecy to ignore.

When discussing the long-expected Battle of Armageddon, one asks where, when, and between whom it will be waged. Questions of a tactical nature are best left to the military men.

Throughout the centuries we have used the name Armageddon to mean any major military conflict involving many nations or in fact, any major decisive conflict at all. Geographically, however, it is the Plain of Megiddo also referred to as the Valley of Jehoshaphat, the fourteen by twenty mile strip of land that runs across Israel from the Mediterranean to the Jordan. Napoleon Bonaparte is reported to have stood on the Mount of Megiddo and remarked, "All of the armies of the world could maneuver for battle here." It is one of the most accessible areas in Israel, for the port of Haifa lies at its western end and makes an ideal supply base.

The biblical prophets place the beginning of this fearsome battle just prior to the second coming of Christ; the same being identified by Nostradamus as the King of Terror who will come to judge the human race. Both spoke of the last great battle which, although not identified by Nostradamus under the name Armageddon, includes the Middle East as the focal point of military strategy.

In my book *Invitation to a Holocaust*, I outlined Nostradamus's battle plan for the Third World War. Being French, he naturally saw the war from the European point of view. The fact that he foresaw some of the major battles taking place in Europe may seem like rather good news for the rest of the world. But the conflict as he sees it will be so immense and so far-reaching that, although much of the killing and bloodshed will take place in Europe, the other parts of the globe will not escape its horrors.

Armageddon: The End of Time?

Close scrutiny of Nostradamus's predictions shows us that the seer expects Israel to be one of the first victims of the Arabs' plan for conquest, conquest not just of the Middle East but all of Europe as well.

With the conflict mounting in Turkey, the defeat of the Greeks, and the breakdown of peace negotiations in Geneva, the stage is being set for the second stage of the war when China hits the West with surprise nuclear attacks and releases frightening bacteriological bombs over Alaska so that the diseases drift on the currents to the countries of the Western Alliance. This will be followed by a Chinese invasion of southern Russia.

Not to be outdone by the Far Eastern powers, the Arabs carry out a battle plan of their own by moving westward and attacking nations in their sphere of influence. Rome will soon be destroyed, civil war will break out in Italy, and France will feel forced to enter the spreading conflict, for by now enemy forces appear to be heading for the French borders.

When the third phase of the war begins, the French will be in the middle of a counteroffensive in Italy, but while they regroup after having been defeated, and while England is becoming the victim of a flood that will devastate the country, the situation in Italy worsens, and the pope will be forced to flee. These events will happen almost simultaneously with the dropping of nuclear bombs on Venice.

During the fourth phase we encounter the total destruction of Monaco, Chinese attacks on France, Chinese and Arab assaults on Spain, and extensive bombing of all of Europe. The fall of Switzerland and the last stand of the Allies near the Belgian city of Bruges will be typical of the long series of defeats that will plague the Allied armies through the first important phases of the war that is to engulf the entire world.

Not until the seventh phase of the war will the United States and Russia finally go on the offensive. Before they do, the easterners will already have moved into Latin America. Although Nostradamus does not predict when the war in the Far East will come to an end, he does state that it will happen when the superpowers begin to use germ warfare on the Chinese and attack them in their home territory.

In the light of international developments, it is extremely interesting that Nostradamus, as far back as the 1500s, gives the Middle Eastern nations a major fighting role in the war. This might seem somewhat implausible in the light of Israel's repeated military victories over its Arab neighbors in recent years, but while the Middle Eastern nations may not appear to be strong now, the next few years will undoubtedly witness a radical change. The Russian influence in the region has been on the decline for a number of years, and U.S. support for Israel is rapidly undermining American influence in that part of the world. By deserting their American and Soviet benefactors in favor of China, the Arabs may find an ally that will have no qualms at all about supplying them with nuclear bombs as well as bacteriological, chemical, and conventional weapons. Once they have built their arsenal, they will strike to the west, China will strike to the south, and the last war will be upon us.

Unlike John of Patmos, Nostradamus does not look at the war as part of a battle between the forces of good and evil. To him it is merely a military operation that will end with the coming of the King of Terror who will act as the Awful Judge.

According to John of Patmos, the Battle of Armageddon will take place when the sixth angel pours out the bowl of wrath upon the River Euphrates in order that the way for the kings of the East might be prepared. The kings of the East are regarded by many interpreters to be the unified armies of Asia under the leadership of Red China. It has been thought that the supernaturally created darkness that will envelop the beast and his kingdom (believed to be the revived Roman Empire), under the fifth plague, will make it possible for the kings of the East to move their army of 200 million (Rev. 9:16) into position close to the banks of the Euphrates, the ancient boundary between the eastern and western empires.

By this time the Euphrates will be dried up, according to the prophecy of John. Interesting in this respect is that this is now entirely possible because of the dam the Russians have constructed near the headwaters of the river.

That Red China can put an army of 200 million in the field should surprise no one. A release written by John Hightower for the Associated Press and datelined April 28, 1964, stated that "The documents [secret Chinese military plans] make clear that the Red Chinese leaders believe they cannot be defeated by long-range nuclear weapons—such as the U.S. missiles—and if they were invaded they would rely on their vast military manpower. One estimate is that in April 1961 there were supposed to be 200 million armed and organized militiamen."

Yet to move 200 million men is a massive undertaking, but with the millions of "expendables" in China that should be no problem. As if following the battle plan for Armageddon and preparing for its destined role, China is already engaged in an ambitious road-building project, constructing a concrete and asphalt ribbon all the way through the Himalayas to Pakistan, ready to move its armies toward the Middle East whenever called for.

Using prophetic material from both John and Daniel—the young Hebrew nobleman who was taken into captivity by King Nebuchadnezzar in 607 B.C., and who left us his prophecies—we find that the first phase of the war begins with the king of the South (Dan. 11:40) staging a massive attack against the Middle East. If this force is to come from the south in relation to Israel, then it has to come from the direction of Arabia and Africa. Simultaneously with the Arab and African attack, the king of the North (USSR?) will move forces into the same region by land and sea. But soon after their arrival, news of troop movements in the East and North (Europe?) cause great anxiety (Dan. 11:44). Advancing on the armies, which are now moving in from two directions, they attack with fury, but even though they try to consolidate their position in and around Jerusalem, they will be defeated. At this point the advancing Chinese hordes will have reached the Euphrates and will be poised to launch their all-out attack on the united armies of the rest of the world.

Tired, still tormented by the effects of the plagues, and suffering the effects of radiation, both armies now begin to fan out all along the sandy lowlands on the eastern shores of the Mediterranean.

Realizing that this will be the showdown of the ages, the leaders will bring the latest weaponry into action, and the most brutal carnage of all times will turn the valley red with blood amid the dying screams of the thousands.

Says John, referring to that battle, "And the winepress was trodden without the city, and blood came out of the winepress, even unto the horses' bridles, by the space of a thousand and six hundred furlongs" (Rev. 14:20).

Imagine—blood to the height of the horses' bridles for two hundred miles!

And suddenly it was all over:

> And there were voices, and thunders, and lightnings; and there was a great earthquake, such as was not since men were upon the earth, so mighty an earthquake, and so great.

> And the great city was divided into three parts,
> and the cities of the nations fell . . .
> And every island fled away, and the mountains were not found. (Rev. 16:18, 19a, 20)

Whether this universal shock wave will be the result of the detonating of all the nuclear warheads or whether it will have a supernatural cause is not certain. What is certain is the major cities of all the nations will be destroyed in an instant and that the earth will be ripped open. Even the mountains and islands will be no more—possibly an indication that we will be dealing with targeted destruction such as that caused by ICBMs. In a conflict such as this I see no reason why the warring nations should not use all the nuclear warheads in their arsenals. The "earthquake" (Greek *seismos*) may well be humanity's very last destructive act, the signal for the Man of Peace to intervene. It has been estimated that by the year 2000 at least fifty nations will have nuclear weapons, possessing between them probably as many as 250,000 warheads. If this ungodly firepower cannot cause a *seismos*, a shaking of the earth, then nothing can!

Even the ancient prophet Isaiah laments:

> Therefore a curse consumes the earth;
> its people must bear their guilt.
> Therefore earth's inhabitants are burned up,
> and very few are left.
> The floodgates of the heavens are opened,
> the foundations of the earth shake.
> The earth is broken up,
> the earth is split asunder,
> the earth is thoroughly shaken.
> The earth reels like a drunkard,

it sways like a hut in the wind.
So heavy on it is the guilt of its rebellion
that it falls—never to rise again. (Isaiah 24:6,
   19–20)

And the Man of Peace? The man Nostradamus called the "great King of Terror" for the wicked, and whom all the others have expected as the "spiritual king" or simply the "savior"? Nostradamus merely expected him. He never saw him in vision.

But the Prophet John did. Amid the mournful cries of the dying and the destruction of a crumbling earth, John looked up:

"And I saw heaven opened, and behold a white horse; and he that sat upon him was called Faithful and True, and in righteousness he doth judge and make war." (Rev. 19:11)

And in majesty he came down to judge the living and raise the dead—exactly the way John predicted.

It *will* happen, and it will take place in just about this way—of that I have no doubt.

But it is the timing that concerns me, for we seem to be in such a desperate rush to come to judgment.

And there is still so much to live for—and A.D. 2000 is already so close. . . .

Epilogue

What do you say after you've just dropped the curtain on a bad play that brought the house down for six thousand years or more—and then finally went broke? Do you apologize to the actors and tell them they weren't bad, but not all that good either? Do you blame the writer for the bad scenes or the meddling director for his constant hassling? Or perhaps the Producer? After all he *is* old, and if it hadn't been for him . . .

Or do you just stop, collect the facts, take a hard look at why it failed and go on from there? After all, there is always hope for the future, isn't there?

In this case there certainly is, strange as it may seem.

Granted, the psychics, prophets, and warmongers have built quite a case for world destruction, and judging from the performance of prophecy in times past and the track record of our own recklessness, chances are that it will all come about as predicted.

But there's a catch. There always is.

While science can see nothing but a dismal future for those who survive the holocaust and the psychics forecast another round of problems even then, the biblical prophets still give hope, both for now and then.

EPILOGUE

For the prophecies about the time of the end are deterministic for our globe, *but they do offer survival for the individual.*

Hope lies in a return to basic values, a strict adherence to the Golden Rule, and the guidelines as laid down in the gentle words of the Beatitudes issued by the greatest Prophet of them all—the true Man of Peace without whom any victory is merely survival.

Bibliography

Aggarwal, Yash P., and Lynn R. Sykes. "Earthquakes, Faults and Nuclear Power Plants in Southern New York and Northern New Jersey," *Science*, April 28, 1978.

Allen, Hugh. *Window in Providence*. Boston: Bruce Humphries, 1943.

Bander, Peter. *The Prophecies of Saint Malachy and Saint Columbkille*. Gerrards Cross, England: Colin Smythe, 1969.

Berlitz, Charles. *Doomsday 1999 A.D.* Garden City, N.Y.: Doubleday, 1981.

Brown, Florence V. *Nostradamus: The Truth about Tomorrow*. New York: Tower, 1970.

Brown, Hugh Auchincloss. *Cataclysms of the Earth*. Boston: Twayne, 1967.

Carter, Mary Ellen. *Edgar Cayce on Prophecy*. New York: Paperback Library, 1968.

Council on Environmental Quality. *Global 2000 Report to the President*. Washington, D.C.: U.S. Government Printing Office, 1980.

Cournos, John, ed. *A Book of Prophecy*. New York: Scribner's, 1942.

BIBLIOGRAPHY

Culleton, R. Gerald. *The Prophets and Our Times.* St. Benedict, Oregon: St. Benedict Press, 1941.

Don, Frank. *Earth Changes Ahead.* New York: Destiny, 1981.

Forman, Henry J. *The Story of Prophecy.* New York: Tudor, 1940.

Gibran, Kahlil. *A Tear and a Smile.* New York: Knopf, 1976.

Glass, Justine. *They Foresaw the Future.* New York, Putnam, 1969.

Goldwater, Barry. *With No Apologies.* New York: Morrow, 1979.

Greenhouse, Herbert B. *Premonitions: A Leap into the Future.* New York: Warner, 1971.

Healy, J. H. and P. Anthony Marshall. "Nuclear Explosions and Distant Earthquakes: A Search for Correlations," *Science,* July 10, 1970.

Hesse, Hermann. *Siddhartha.* 1922. Reprint, New York: Bantam, 1951.

Laver, James. *Nostradamus.* London: Penquin, 1952.

Ley, Willy. *On Earth and in the Sky.* New York: Ace, 1962.

Lindsey, Hal. *There's a New World Coming.* Eugene, Oregon: Harvest House, 1973.

Logan, Daniel. *The Reluctant Prophet.* New York: Avon, 1968.

The Lost Books of the Bible and the Forgotten Books of Eden. 1926. Reprint, New York: New American Library, 1974.

MacArthur, Douglas. *Reminiscences.* New York: McGraw-Hill, 1964.

Marchi, John de. *The True Story of Fatima.* St. Paul: Catechetical Guild Educational Society, 1956.

Migne, Jacques Paul, *Patrologia Graeca.* Paris: Vol. 107.

Morfill, W. R. *The Book of the Secrets of Enoch.* Oxford: Clarendon Press, 1896.

National Tribune, December 1880.

Noone, Richard W. *Ice, the Ultimate Disaster.* Dunwoody, G. A.: Genesis, 1982.

Noorbergen, Rene. *The Death Cry of an Eagle.* Grand Rapids, Mich.: Zondervan, 1980.

———. *Ellen G. White, Prophet of Destiny.* New Canaan, Conn.: Keats, 1972.

———. *Invitation to a Holocaust.* London: New English Library, 1981.

———. *Jeane Dixon—My Life & Prophecies.* New York: Morrow, 1970.

———. *The Soul Hustlers.* Grand Rapids, Mich.: Zondervan, 1976.

O'Brien, M. J. *An Historical and Critical Account of the So-called Prophecy of St. Malachy Regarding the Secession of the Popes.* Dublin: O'Brien, 1880.

Ozanne, C. G. *The First Seven Thousand Years.* New York: Exposition, 1970.

Ponte, Lowell. *The Cooling.* Englewood Cliffs, N.J.: Prentice-Hall, 1976.

Robb, Stewart. *Prophecies on World Events by Nostradamus.* New York: Liveright, 1961.

Roberts, Henry, C. *The Complete Prophecies of Nostradamus.* New York: Nostradamus, 1949.

Roerich, Nicholas. *Altai-Himalaya.* New York: Frederick Stokes, 1929.

St. Hilaire, Josephine. *On Eastern Crossroads.* New York: Frederick Stokes, 1930.

"San Andreas Fault Found Shifting at Rapid Rate," *New York Times*, June 19, 1978.

BIBLIOGRAPHY

Starr, Douglas. "How Climate Might Shift in Next 1,000 Years," *Christian Science Monitor*, February 14, 1976.

Taylor, Ronald A. "The Plague That's Killing America's Trees," *U.S. News & World Report*, April 23, 1984.

Velikovsky, Immanuel. *Earth in Upheaval*. Garden City, N.Y.: Doubleday, 1955.

Velikovsky, Immanuel. *Worlds in Collision*. Garden City, N.Y.: Doubleday, 1950.

Von Dollinger, John. *Prophecies and the Prophetic Spirit in the Christian Era*. London: Rivingstons, 1873.

Walvoord, John F. *Israel in Prophecy*. Grand Rapids, Mich.: Zondervan, 1962.

Ward, Charles. *Oracles of Nostradamus*. New York: Scribner's, 1940.

White, Ellen G. *The Great Controversy*. Oakland, Calif.: Pacific Press, 1888.

White, John. *Pole Shift*. Garden City, N.Y.: Doubleday, 1980.

Willoya, William, and Vinson Brown. *Warriors of the Rainbow*. Healdsburg, Calif.: Naturegraph, 1962.

Wilson, Dwight. *Armageddon Now*. Grand Rapids, Mich.: Baker, 1977.

"The Wobbling Earth," *Science News*, August 14, 1971.

INDEX

A

Accuracy of psychic predictions, 35–36, 135–38
Acid rain, 65–69
Ackerman, Thomas P., 130
Adams, Henry, 6
Adwattan, 8–9
Africa
  impact of 1755 earthquake on, 108–9
  threat of locusts in, 120
Agneya weapon, 8–9
"Agony signals" of plant, 77–79
Air quality, 63. See also Pollution
Alamogordo, New Mexico, 7
Alaskan quake of 1964, 96
Allah, 6
Allen, Hugh, 92
Ambonese, 21
American-Israel Public Affairs Committee, 2
American Revolution, 33. See also Washington, George, vision of
Andhakas, 8, 9

Animals
  danger of pollution to, 73
  predictive senses of, 96
Annihilation, man-made threat of. See Nuclear war
Antarctica, polar shift and, 98
Antichrist
  Child of East as, 50–51
  coming of, 44
  humanity's choice concerning, 56
Antigod of Ikhnaton, 50
Anxiety about future, 1–0. See also Armageddon
Apocalyptic writings. See John of Patmos
Aquarian eclipse conjunction, 49
Arghati, mystical tradition of, 18–19
Armageddon, 141–50
  Battle of, 144–50
  fear of, 140
  Isaiah's predictions of, 149–50
  John of Patmos' predictions of, 123, 146–149
  Nostradamus' predictions of, 144–46

INDEX

Armageddon—Cont.
  nuclear war and, 143–44, 146–47, 149
  use of name, 144
Armagh, Saint Malachy of, 23–24, 134
Astrology, Nostradamus' use of, 37
Atlantis, sinking of, 20
Atmosphere
  carbon dioxide levels in, 69
  consequences of nuclear war to, 130–32
  ozone layer, 71
Atomic-bomb. *See also* Nuclear war
  biblical prophecies of, 143
  possibility of ancient detonation of, 7–10
Aton, religion of, 50
Australia, deforestation in, 75
Avatar, 19–20
Aztecs, beliefs about world leader, 25–26

B

Backster, Cleve, 77–79
Backster Research Foundation, 77
Bacon, Roger, 14
Barnabas, Epistle of, 40, 41
Bartsch, Paul, 70
Bavarian Forest, acid rain's effect on, 68
Beirut, massacre of Marines in, 2
Belshazzar, King, xi
Bergstrom, Sune K., 129
Bernhard, Prince of Netherlands, 73
Biblical chronology, 40–42
Biblical prophecies. *See also* specific prophets
  accuracy of, 138
  of atomic-bomb, 143
  of end of world, 99
  escaping wrath of, 139
  Reagan's concern over, 2
Black Forest, Germany, acid rain's effect on, 67–68
Blavatsky, Madame, 89
Boristhenes, Nostradamus' use of, 15–16
Bradshaw, Wesley, 28
Brazil, deforestation in, 74
Brower, Kenneth, 67
Brown, Hugh Auchincloss, 98
Bruck, Robert, 66
Brueggeman, Walter, 76
Buddha, reincarnation of, 17–18
Buddhists, predictions of, 133
Bull, Colin, 97
Byrd Antarctic Expedition, 98

C

Calcutta, India, population of, 72
California, San Andreas Fault in, 94
California, University of, 61
Canada, acid rain in, 67
Cancer
  damage to ozone layer and, 71
  incidence in U.S., 63
Carbon dioxide in atmosphere, 69
Carter, James Earl, 127
Catherine de Medicis, Nostradamus and, 39
Cayce, Edgar, 85, 86
  on Child of East's birth, 49
  on destruction of Europe, 86–87
  on geological changes, 85, 86, 89, 93
  "spiritual rebirth" prediction, 12
Celestine II, 23
Central Telegram Bureau of International Astronomical Union, 82
Centuries, Les (Nostradamus), 37, 42
"Chance prediction", 138
Charles IX, Nostradamus and, 39
Chesapeake Bay, pollution in, 64
Child of East, 46–58
  birth of, 46–49, 51, 52
  Dixon's revelation of, 46–48, 50–57

Index

Child of East—Cont.
   as imitation Son of God, 50–51
   similarity to Christ, 51, 52–53
China
   Battle of Armageddon and, 145–47
   deforestation in, 74–75
Christ
   birth of, 49
   in John of Patmos' vision, 104–5
   prophecies of his return, 22–23, 43–44
   similarity to Child of East, 51, 52–55
Christianity diminished influence of, 54
Christianization of Russia, 12–13
Christians
   belief in world leader, 22–24
   predictions of, 133
Chronology, biblical, 40–42
Churchill, Winston, 11
CIA, 76–78
Climatic changes, fossil fuels and, 69
Coal fuel, acid rain and, 67, 68
Collective memory, 51
Comet collisions, 82–83, 118–19
Commoner, Barry, 61
Communications systems of living cells, 77–79
Communism, literary ancestors of, 14
"Conditional prophecy", 138–39
Cooling, The (Ponte), 80
Cornell University, 65, 130
Cosgrove, West, 127
Council on Economic Priorities, 128
"Creature comforts", effects of, 71
Criswell, 92

D

Dalai lama, 18
Daniel (seer), 79, 103, 138, 147
DDT, overuse of, 70–71
Deforestation, 74–75

Deganawida, predictions of, 27
D'Estaing, Valery Giscard, 142
Destruction, predictions of, 58–100
   by comets and meteors, 82–85, 118
   DDT, overuse of, 70–71
   earth wobble, 81, 97–100
   environmental pollution, 61–79
   in Europe, 86–87, 89
   by geological alterations, 80–100
   in Great Britain, 88–91
   industry and, 61–69
   overpopulation, 71–79
   in South Pacific, 85–86
   in U.S., 91–95
Dijkshoorn, M.D., 137
Dikshitar, V.R., 7
Dine, Thomas, 2
Dixon, Jeane, 45–48
   accuracy of, 35–36, 137
   comet prediction of, 82
   forecasting coming of Antichrist, 44
   manner of revelations, 104
   predictions, summary of, 133
   revelation of Child of East, 46–48, 50–57
Djojobojo, 21
Dnieper, Nostradamus' predictions about, 14–16
Domitian, emperor, 103
Don, Frank, 74
Dubridge, Lee A., xiii, 61
Dykman, Clarence, 45

E

Earth Changes Ahead (Don), 74
Earthquakes
   frequency of, 80–81
   great, of 1755, 108–9
   prediction of, 86–87
   theory of plate tectonics and, 94–95
Earth wobble, 81, 97–100
Ecosystem, pollution of, 64–65

INDEX

Egypt
   Child of East in, 49, 53
   Ikhnaton's reign of, 50
Einstein, Albert, 97, 142
End of life, possibility of, 1–10
England
   Mother Shipton's predictions of, 16
   Nostradamus' prediction of flooding of, 88–91
Enoch, book of, 40–41
Environment, misuse of. See Pollution
Epistle to Henri II (Nostradamus), 43
Eschatologists, 138
Eskimos, DDT rate in, 71
Etna, Mount, 86
Euphrates, River, 146–47
Europe, predictions of destruction of, 86–87, 89
Exit, 126
Extermination of mammals, 65
Extinction, Watt's prediction of, 61

F

Famine as a result of comet hitting Indian Ocean, 119
Far East, evidence of ancient atomic explosion in, 10
Fatima, Portugal, prediction given in, 12–13
Fear of future, 1–10. See also Armageddon
February 5, 1962, significance of, 46–50
Fiesole, Italy, 87
Flood predictions of Nostradamus, 87–91
Fluorocarbons, 71. See also Pollution
Forests
   destruction of, 74–75
   effect of pollution on, 66, 67–68
Forgotten race of men, 6–7

Fossil fuel
   acid rain and, 67, 68
   climatic changes from burning of, 69
Four Horsemen, vision of, 105–7
Four trumpets prophecy, 117–19
French seer. See Nostradamus
Friede, Johann, 81–82

G

Gannon, James, 67
Gautama Buddha, 15–16
Gavin, Jim, 92
Genghis Khan, 44
Geological changes, predictions of, 80–100
   comets and meteors, 82–85
   earth wobble, 81, 86–87
   in Europe, 86–87, 89
   in Great Britain, 88–91
   in South Pacific, 85–86
   in U.S., 91–95
Germany, Black Forest of, 67–68
Ghurka, 9
Gift of Prophecy, A (Montgomery), 55
Giovinetto, 97
Glaciers, meltwater from, 84
Global 2000 Report, 127
"Global Atmospheric Consequences of Nuclear War" (Sagan, Toon, Ackerman, Pollack & Turco), 130
Global wobbling, 81, 97–100
Goebbels, Joseph, 36
Great Britain
   belief in psychic phenomena in, 5
   Nostradamus' prediction of flooding of, 88–91
   use of Nostradamian prophecies in World War I, 36
Great earthquake, the, 108–9
Greeks, predictions of worldwide cataclysm by, 20
Guide to Self-Deliverance, A (Exit), 126

Index

Guiness Book of World Records, The (McWhirter brothers), 72

H

Hamburg, Germany, 68
Harappa, evidence of ancient atomic explosion in, 10
Harmony in end-of-time visions, 58
Hartung, Bill, 128
Heraclitus of Ephesus, 20, 133
Hermes Trismegistus, 4
Hesse, Germany, 68
Hightower, John, 147
Hildegard, Saint, 51
Hindus, predictions of, 19–20, 133
Hiroshima, 10, 144
Hitler, Adolf, 36
Hobbs, William, 92
Holland, Kenneth J., 60
Hopi Indians, predictions of, 26, 133
Hughes, Irene, 104
Hurkos, Peter, 137

I

Ice, deposition of, 97–99
Ice, the Ultimate Disaster (Noone), 98
Ikhnaton, 46–47, 48, 50, 55
India
   Calcutta, population of, 72
   Mahabharata of, 7–10
   Indian Ocean, predictions of comet hitting, 118–19
   Indonesians, predictions of, 21
   Industry, pollution caused by, 61–69
   Innocent II, Pope, 23, 24
   Inquisition, era of, 38, 39
International Astronomical Union, Central Telegram Bureau of, 82

International Wildlife (magazine), 73
Interpretation of Radium (Soddy), 6–7
Invitation to a Holocaust (Noorbergen), 144
Iran, Zoastrian Vestas of, 22
Iraq, evidence of ancient atomic explosion in, 10
Ireland, evidence of ancient atomic explosion in, 10
Iroquois Indians, predictions of, 26–27, 133
Isaiah, Battle of Armageddon and, 149–150

J

Jaag, Otto, 62
Japan
   Indonesia and, 21
   predictions of destruction in, 86
Jeane Dixon—My Life & Prophecies (Noorbergen), 45, 82
Jehoshapat, Valley of, 144
Jerusalem, Antichrist headquarters in, 55
Jesus of Nazareth
   birth of, 49
   in John of Patmos' vision, 104–5
   prophecies of return, 22–23, 43–44
   similarity to Child of East, 51, 52–55
Jews, predictions of, 134
Joel, the prophet, 103
John of Patmos, visions of, 101–23
   accuracy of, 138
   on Battle of Armageddon, 146–49
   concern of, 103
   darkest day in history, 110–12
   great earthquake, 108–9
   manner of reception, 104–5
   moon turning to blood, 112–13

161

INDEX

rain of stars, 113–16
seven seals, 105–8
seven trumpets, 117–23
vision of Man of Peace, 150
warnings of, 99–100
Johnsson, Olaf, 137
John the Apostle, prediction of, 64
John the Baptist, 54
Judgment, humanity's rush to, 125–40
Jupiter, Saturn's conjunction with, 49–50

K

Kahlil Gibran, 35, 125
Kalki, 20
Kauravas, 8
Kavan, Father, 55
Kennedy, Leigh Ann, 126
Kepler, Johannes, 49
Kiev, 15
Krakatoa, eruption of, 80–81

L

La Rogue, Cardinal, 23
Lateran Council, 23
Latin America
 deforestation in, 74–75
 Montezuma's vision and, 25–26
"Law of More", 13, 14
Leader, rise of last world, 11–34
 Aztec belief, 25–26
 Buddha reincarnation, 17–18
 Christian belief, 22–24
 Gautama Buddha's predictions of, 15–16
 Greek beliefs, 20
 Hindu belief, 19–20
 Indonesian belief, 21
 John of Patmos' vision of, 150
 North American Indians belief, 26–27
 Tibetan beliefs, 18–19
 Washington's vision of, 27–34, 135
 Zoastrian belief, 22, 135
Leoni, Edgar, 14
Leo VI, Emperor, 23

Let Me Die before I Wake, 126
Life and Death of Planet Earth, The (Valentine), 97
Lignum Vitae (Wion), 24
Lijinski, William, 63
Likens, Gene E., 65
Lisbon, Portugal, great earthquake of, 108–9
Locusts, threat of, 120
Lofoten Islands, evidence of ancient atomic explosion in, 10
Logan, Daniel, 48–49, 104, 134, 137

M

MacArthur, Douglas, 139–40
McWhirter brothers, 72
Madhi, 22
Mahabharata, 7–10, 127, 143
Maitreya (World Unifier), 17–18
Malachy, Saint, prophecies of, 23–24, 134
Mammals, extermination of, 65
Manhattan Project, 7
Man of East, 54
Man of Peace. *See* Leader, rise of last world
Marines, massacre in Beirut of, 2
Marsden, Brian, 82
Marx, Karl, 15
Maryland, University of, students at, 60
Mass, Malthasar, 89
Matthew
 Book of, xii
 predictions of, 107, 143
Mediterranean area, predictions of destruction, 86–87
Megiddo, Plain of, 144
Memory, collective, 51
Messiah, 22. *See also* Jesus of Nazareth
Meteors
 collisions, geological alterations from, 83–85
 rain of stars prophecy, 114–16
Mexico, deforestation in, 75
Michener, James, 58–59
Middle Ages, supernatural in, 23

Index

Middle East
  Battle of Armageddon and, 145–46, 148
  future of, 5–6
  revelation of Child of East's birth in, 46–49
  threat of locusts in, 120
Military establishment, biblical prophecies and, 141–42
Millenium theory, Sabbath, 40–43
Miller, G. Tylor, 59
Mission of Child of East, 53–54
Mohenjo-Daro, evidence of ancient atomic explosion in, 10
Molukkers, 21
Mongols, Nostradamus' predictions and, 44
Montezuma, vision of, 25–26, 134
Montgomery, Ruth, 55
Moon, John of Patmos' prophecy of, 112–13
More, Sir Thomas, 14, 15
Mortara, Italy, 90
Moscow, Russia, 16
Muhammad, Prophet, 22–23
Munich, University, 68
Muslims, predictions of, 22, 134
Myers, Norman, 73

N

Nagasaki, 10, 144
Napoleon, Bonaparte, 144
National Academy of Science, 68–69
National Aeronautics and Space Administration, 69, 130
National Institute for Occupational Safety and Health, 63
National Tribune, 27, 28
Nature (magazine), 94
Nebuchadnezzar, King, 147
Nefertiti, Queen, 46–47, 48, 50, 52
Nelson, Robert, 137
New England, extraordinary darkness over, 111–12
Newsweek (magazine), 126

New Testament, prophecies of, 102
New York City, destruction of, 91–94
New York Journal of Commerce, 114
New York Times, 120
1984 (Orwell), xi
Noone, Richard W., 98
Norsemen, prophecies of, 4
North American Indians, traditions involving Man of Peace, 26–27
North Carolina University, 66
Nostradamus, 13–16, 33–45
  accuracy of, 136
  calculations, 42–43
  coding of predictions, 38, 39
  comet and meteor prediction, 82–83
  on destruction of Europe, 86–87
  on destruction of N.Y.C., 91–92
  on final armed conflict, 39–45
  flood predictions, 86–91
  last great battle predicted by, 134, 144–46
  life of, 37–39
  manner of revelations, 104
  on Russia, 13–14
  similarities to John of Patmos, 118
  sources of visions, 37–38
  South Pacific disaster prediction, 85–86
  use of by Goebbels, 36
Nostredame, Michel de. *See* Nostradamus
Nuclear arms race, 126–27, 142
Nuclear war, 126–32
  fear of, 126–27
  possibility of, 3
  Armageddon and, 143–44, 146–47, 149
  effects of, 129–32

O

Occult, Hitler's belief in, 36
Oglala Sioux, traditions of, 26, 134

163

INDEX

Old Testament, prophecies of, 102
Olmsted, Denison, 115
Olympus, Mount, 87
Omni (magazine), 67
Oppenheimer, Robert, 7
Oracles, Sibylline, 4
Orwell, George, xi
"Ostrich syndrome", 60
Ouranoi, 143
Overein, Lars, N., 67
Overpopulation, 71–79
Ozone layer, 71

P

Pakistan, evidence of ancient atomic explosion in, 10
Palestine Liberation Army, 5
Pandavas, 8
Patmos, John of. *See* John of Patmos, visions of
PCB, 62
Pendragon, John, 89, 93
Peter, predictions of, 143
Philip, Prince, Duke of Edinburgh, 73
Pius XI, Pope, 24
Plagues, John of Patmos' vision of seven, 121–24
Plant life, sensitivity of, 77–79
Plate tectonics, theory of, 94–95
Plato, 14, 20
Pole shift, 96–100
Pollack, James B., 130
Pollution, 61–79
  acid rain, 65–69
  DDT overuse, 70–71
  effect of comet hitting Indian Ocean, 119
  industry and, 61–69
  overpopulation, 71–79
Ponte, Lowell, 80, 81
Population, increasing, 71–79
Pravda, Czechoslovakia, 68
Predestination, 6
Predictive techniques for earthquakes, 95–96

Prophecy. *See also* Armageddon; specific prophets
  common time period of, 4
  conditional, vs. chance prediction, 138–139
  correlation between world events and, xii
Prophetia de Futuris Ponificibus Romanis (St. Malachy), 23
Psychic phenomena, 4–5
Psychic predictions
  accuracy of, 135–38
  comparing, 132–36

R

R & D Associates, 130
Ragnarok of Norsemen, 4
Rain, acid, 65–69
Rain of stars, 113–16
Raleigh, North Carolina, 66
Reagan, Ronald, 1–2
Red China, army of, 147
Reincarnation
  of Buddha, 17–18
  of Vishnu, 20
Reluctant Prophet, The (Logan), 48
Republic (Plato), 14
Revelation. *See also* John of Patmos
  manner of, 104
  prophecies in, 44, 45
Rhine River, pollution of, 62
Rhone River, pollution of, 62–63
Riesenman, Regis, 136
Ring of Fire, 80, 86, 118
Robb, Steward, 14
Robinson, 97
Rochester, University of, 7
Roper survey, 5
Ross Sea, 98
Rotterdam, pollution in, 63
Russia, forecasts about, 11–16

S

Sabbath millennium theory, 40–43

Index

Sagan, Carl, 130–32
Sahara Desert
  deforestation in, 75
  evidence of ancient atomic explosion in, 10
Sahel, deforestation in, 75
Saint Helens, Mount, eruption of, 80
St. Thomas High School, Houston, Texas, 127
Sakharov, Andrei, 142–43
San Andreas Fault, 94
Saoshyant, 22
Satan, White's vision of, 57
Saturn, Jupiter's conjunction with, 49–50
Schiffer, Robert, 69
Schutt, Peter, 68
Science, progress of, 6
Scotland
  evidence of ancient atomic explosion in, 10
  Nostradamus' prediction of flooding of, 88–89
Seals, seven, 105–8
Sears, Robert, 108
Seed banks, deforestation and, 75
Seven seals, 105–8
Seven trumpets, 117–23
Shepherd, Jack, 64
Sherman, Anthony, 28
Sherman, Harold, 137
Shipton, Mother, 16, 134
Sibylline oracles, 4
Siddhartha, Prince, 16–17
Sinking Ark, The (Myers), 73
"Sleeping seer". *See* Cayce, Edgar
Smithsonian Institution, 65
Snedeker, Edward, 137
Snow Accumulation in Antarctica (Bull), 97
Soddy, Frederick, 6–7
Soul Hustlers, The (Noorbergen), 135
South, Penny, 137
South America, earthquakes and tidal waves predicted for, 94
South Pacific, predictions of disaster in, 85–86

Soviet Union
  forecasts about, 11–16
  Nostradamus predictions about, 13–14
  Tabas, Iran earthquake and, 93–94
Spiritualization in Russia, 12
Stalin, Joseph, 12
Stars, rain of, 113–16
Stars and Stripes, 27
Stowe, Leland, 140
Strange Prophecies That Came True (Robb), 14
Strong, Robert, 137
Sukarno, 21
Sun, John of Patmos' prophecy of, 110–12
Supernatural guidance in world affairs, 27–34
Swan, Ingel, 137
Switzerland, pollution in, 62–63
Syria, Child of East in, 53

T

Tabas, Iran, earthquake in, 93–94
T'ang-shan, China, earthquake in, 95
TAPPS report, 130
Technology, environmental disease and, 61–69
Tectonics, plate, 94–95
These Times, 60
Third World, condition of, xii
Third World War, 144–50
Thomas, Eugene, 62
Tibetans, prophecies of world leader, 18–19, 135
Time (magazine), 67
Time of end, 1–10
  predictions of, 4–5
Togliatti, East Germany, 68
Toon, Owen B., 130
Tropical forests, wildlife in, 73–74
True Centuries, The (Nostradamus), 45
Trumpets, seven, 117–23
Turco, Richard P., 130
Tutankhamon, 50

INDEX

U

U.S. Department of Agriculture, 70
U.S. Environmental Protection Agency, 64, 68
U.S. Mariner spacecraft, 129–30
Ukraine, Nostradamus' predictions about, 14–16
Underdeveloped countries, increase in population, 72
United Arab Republic, Child of East in, 53
United Nations, 61
United States
  belief in psychic phenomena in, 5
  birth of, 27–28
  deforestation in, 75
  destruction in, 91–95
  incidence of cancer in, 63
  pollution in, 63–67
  spending for nuclear warheads, 127
  support of Child of East, 54
  toxic substance list, 62
  war games, 128–29
  Washington's vision of future of, 27–34, 135
Uranium, derivation of word, 143
Utopia (More), 14

V

Valdai Hill, 15–16
Valentine, Manson, 70
Valentine, Tom, 97
Valley Forge, Washington's vision at, 28–33
Varro, calculations of, 42
Velikovsky, Immanuel, 83–84
Virgin Mary, prediction given by, 12–13
Vishnu, reincarnation of, 20
Volcanic eruptions
  frequency of, 80–81
  predictions of, 86–87
Vrishnis, 8, 9

W

Ward, Charles A., 90
War games, 128–29
Washington, George, vision of, 27–34, 135
Watt, Kenneth E.F., 61
Weapons in *Mahabharata*, 8–10. *See also* Nuclear war
Weather conditions, meteor's impact upon, 84–85
Webster, Noah, 110
Westminster Abbey, 90–91
Wheatstone bridge, 77, 78
While Time Remains (Stowe), 140
White, Ellen G., 57–58
William, Samuel, 111
Wilson, J. Tuzo, 94–95
Window in Providence (Allen), 92
Wion, Arnold, 24
Wobble, earth, 81, 97–100
World affairs, supernatural guidance in, 27–34
World events, correlation between prophecy and, xii
World Health Organization, 129
World leader. *See* Leader, rise of last world
World Unifier (Maitreya), 17–18
World War I, 142
World War II, 128, 142
World Wildlife Fund, 73

Y

Yom Kippur War of 1973, 142
Yudistthira, 9

Z

Zarathustra, 22
Zechariah, predictions of, 143–44
Zoastrian Vestas of Iran, 22, 135
Zurich, Lake of, 62
Zurich Canton, 62

166